MESSAGES FROM
Heaven

How Visions and Wonder Rescued a
Handicapped Boy who went on to
Write 14 Books and Give us all
"Messages from Heaven"

Deacon Eddie Ensley, Ph.D.

Praise for *Messages from Heaven*

The first and most basic definition of a miracle refers to something that seems so extraordinary that it captures our attention and fills us with a sense of wonderment at what God has done and is doing in our lives and in our world each and every day. In *Messages from Heaven*, Eddie Ensley invites us to realize that God, through Jesus Christ and in the Holy Spirit, constantly infuses our lives biographically and experientially with such wonders. Deacon Ensley effectively shows us how to recover not only that sense of the sacredness of daily living forever engraved in our world by the incarnation itself but also and especially that sense of wonderment that really pervades "ordinary" daily life, if we are but attentive enough to recognize and to realize that God continues his revelatory self-disclosure in making the extraordinary come to life every day in what first seems merely "ordinary."

—Reverend Msgr. Christopher J. Schreck, PhD, STD
Rector/President Pontifical College Josephinum

God rewrites the gospel in the life of every believer, but few of us take down the dictation. Eddie Ensley has done so and shares his journey in *Messages from Heaven*. Looking for a boost in your faith life? Walk through these pages with Eddie.

— Fr. George T. Montague, theologian, author,
St. Mary's University

I have shared my testimony about coming to Jesus Christ, and becoming a Catholic in public thousands of times. But I always hold back some of the more personal revelations God has given me. Eddie Ensley takes a bold step in revealing his more personal encounters with Christ to strengthen those who listen. Thank you, Deacon Eddie, for the courage to share!

—**John Michael Talbot,** author and musician

It has been my privilege to personally know Eddie Ensley for the past 40 years. I can attest that he is a person who truly enters into prayerful intimacy with the living God. We are fortunate that through this book Eddie has at long last chosen to reveal his own deeply touching personal story. Moreover, he shares the tender loving comfort and encouragement he received as he listened with an open heart to Messages from Heaven.

— **Dominic Berardino**
President, Southern California Renewal Communities (SCRC)
Archdiocese of Los Angeles

Deacon Eddie's personal stories of encountering the love of God in the darkest of times, will bring hope to the hopeless and courage to face daily life afresh. I hope you will be as encouraged as I was.

— **Dan Almeter**, LMFT marriage and family
therapist, head of Alleluia Catholic Fellowship,
Alleluia Community, Augusta GA

DEDICATION

This book is dedicated to my pastor and friend Fr. Jeremiah McCarthy, a wonderful human being and a wonderful pastor who has touched my life with his balance and wisdom.

ACKNOWLEDGMENTS

Many thanks to Patrice Fagnant-MacArthur, my private editor of the book, for her wonderful suggestions and help on the structure of the book, copy-editing, and support.

And also with appreciation for Joanna Brunson and Dr. Susan Sendalbach for reading and commenting on the book as it was in progress.

Contents

Introduction

As I sat in the conference room with six other people, I was about to hear some astounding things. It was the church office of a large parish in the Midwest. Deacon Robert Herrmann and I had just finished a mission at this parish and the staff wanted a retreat the following day. One of the things I talked about is the wondrous, how heaven is nearer to each of us than we dare believe. One by one I gave the staff members a chance to respond.

One middle-aged woman, the accountant, started off, reluctantly at first but with growing confidence as she spoke. She said, "My family has experienced the wondrous, too." She told about a time when she was a little girl in a house full of six children. One of the older boys had been out delivering papers and had not been home in time for supper. Everyone was worried. In about thirty minutes, they were going to start a search for him. He was usually so punctual. As the mother mulled this over alone in her bedroom, she felt a sense of the holy take her over. With her eyes wide open, she saw the glowing figure of an angel. The angel said, "Your son has come home to be with God. Don't be afraid. He's okay and the grace of Jesus will be with you."

A hard knock came at their door a few minutes later. The mother knew instinctively it was a policeman. Her son, who had been riding a bike, had been hit by a car while delivering the papers in town. The loss was terrible but was softened by the experience of the mother which she shared with her family. The story of this had only been told within the family. We were all in amazement. Tears trickled down the accountant's eyes: tears of wonder, tears of God's intimacy, and tears of loss for her brother who would not come back.

The pastor spoke and told us something he had previously shared only with his spiritual director and a couple other special people. When he was a young man of seventeen and struggling with the idea of whether to go to seminary, he dreamed a very spiritual dream in which Christ came up to him, put one hand on each shoulder, and simply said, "Come, follow me." This confirmed his inner leanings and the encouragement from his family and priests to go onto seminary.

As we went around the room, each person had some wondrous story of God's working in their life. Such events do not happen just to saints or holy people in history. Through the Holy Spirit, they happen to ordinary people like you and me.

Many People Have Visions or Mystical Experiences

This is backed up by a study that shows in one Midwestern town many churchgoers have had a major mystical experience. Rev. Ben Johnson, a Lutheran minister with a doctorate in theology from Harvard, and sociologist Milo Brekke surveyed two thousand Christians in mainline churches in St. Cloud, Minnesota. They found that 30 percent had seen dramatic visions, heard heavenly voices, or experienced prophetic dreams. Johnson told a joint meeting of the Society of Biblical Literature and the American Academy of Religion, "Two centuries after the intellectual world has said that these kinds of things do not happen, they show up among almost a third of the population in a conservative Midwestern city."[1]

Recently, on the retreats I've given, I've shared more of my story of growing up, zeroing in especially on God's grace and movements, his touch in my life, which helped me to overcome seemingly impossible hurtles. I also told of the pain and suffering of those times when I needed such a warm touch from God's love to enable me to continue.

The effect on the audiences has been dramatic. A lot of healing has taken place in people. There have been tears of gladness, joy, and repentance. I feel it is now time to write a book that talks about what I must simply call my visions and messages from a heart I pray was touched by God. I know such things are mediated; they come through my humanity, from my unconscious, from the things I've read, and from the people I've talked to. This raw material is, I pray, touched and rearranged by the Holy Spirit. To paraphrase St. Thomas Aquinas, it is grace building on the natural.[2]

I Struggled with a Disability

I tell the story of how I struggled throughout my childhood from a major neurological and motor disability, likely caused by a birth injury. I also relate how I lived in a dysfunctional home where things could turn dangerous in an instant. The prospects of a fulfilled life seemed remote. Then, repeatedly, God startled me with his Presence. These spiritual experiences calmed me, infused me with a sense of wonder, and prepared and called me to a ministry of writing many books and preaching to hundreds of thousands of people.

Through these vivid encounters, messages formed in my soul which I yearned to share. This book is part of that sharing. It takes a nuanced look at visions and spiritual experiencing, borrowing understanding from medieval women visionaries and mystics, patristic sources, and my own American Indian culture. It can help to open all of us to the touch of God.

People are hesitant, even afraid, today to freely share or write about their touches of wonder. That is the mindset we too often encounter even in the Church today, but the Church once viewed things very differently. It realized that visions happened to normal people.

An example of this is found in the thousands of accounts of healing that were recorded at the time they happened. It is a vast body of literature theologians have yet to fully consider. Whenever someone experienced a healing, they would go to a shrine to give thanks. The story of the healing would be written in a book, sometimes called the *Book of Miracles*. In the Middle Ages, those healed would often testify under oath and be cross-examined. Very often visions played a role in their healing. They would be led by a dream to pray for healing at a shrine where they were told the healing would take place. These are not invented saints' legends, but what people experienced as they went about their normal lives.

For example, St. Augustine in *The City of God* gives a long account of many such happenings in his own parish that occurred throughout his tenure as bishop and pastor.[3] Another book, *Dreams, Visions, and Spiritual Authority in Merovingian Gaul,* is the source of hundreds of stories. Medieval historians use those stories to find out what daily life was like when those people lived. We also read about such accounts in the lives of saints from this period.

Modern theologians too quickly branded those accounts as novels or pious fiction. However, when you look at the fact that such events were happening daily among ordinary people as these books of miracles show, these accounts become very believable and not so easy to dismiss. Historical research can not necessarily prove these healings occurred, but it does verify that people believed they experienced the wondrous and perceived that they and those around them had visions.

Our Heritage is Full of God's Wonder in People's Lives

The great spiritual writers and mystics of the Church often shared such experiences. Augustine wrote of his own visions and the visions of his parish in Hippo. Other men like Thomas á Kempis also wrote great visionary literature, but women were most often the authors of these works.

For a thousand years, from late antiquity to the 15th century, women wrote about their encounters with God. Written by hermits, recluses, wives, mothers, wandering teachers, founders of religious communities, and reformers, these women wrote powerful devotional literature telling of their visions in a way that captured both head and heart. Prominent among these were Catherine of Siena, Hildegard of Bingen, Juliana of Norwich, and Mechthild of Magdeburg. People who read or listened to those accounts were caught up in wonder and experienced that same wonder in their own lives. Such accounts disclose mystery, the seemingly unknowable, and the wondrous that is behind all creation.

Our ancestors understood the subtle interrelationships of flesh and spirit more accurately than we do. They looked for the touch of visions in their daily lives. When they heard of visions, they knew what to do with them. Visionary literature consisted of heart-mending imagery and was connected to the subterranean depth of the soul, forming a symphony of God's intimacy and love. This genre of writing once wonderfully enriched the whole of society. Isn't it time for contemporary spiritual writers to share their experiences and write in that genre again?

Scientists have shown that we are hardwired for God, that our brains are built for spiritual experiencing.[4] Such spiritual experiencing once enhanced human life and people felt able to talk about it freely. We too often have thought of such events as happening only to saints because we find them in saints' lives. In reality, those saints lived in a period when such experiences were commonly reported and talked about. Such experiences, I believe, can be an experience of God; even a miraculous experience.

At the same time, these experiences are not hotlines to heaven. They are mediated. These experiences are part God and part us. They come through the images of our unconscious. They come through the things we've read, the things we believe, our experiences in life, as well as God working in our lives. In short, I believe they are a touch of the Holy Spirit moving within our humanness rather than totally other and supernatural.

Another mistake that we make in our culture, in the Church even, is to brand such experiences as rare. When they do happen we call them supernatural, breaking the laws of nature. The word "supernatural" has a purpose, but it is not the word I'm most comfortable with when describing my own experience.

Miracles and Visions are Both Natural and Wondrous

Before the 16th century, our ancestors in faith did not divide the world into the natural and the supernatural. The idea of miracles as breaking natural law was unknown to them. Miracles and visions were both natural and wondrous. They may have gone contrary to the normal course of nature, but they were still natural. In a way, this is a far more sophisticated way of looking at visions than we have today. Miracles and visions were events that provoked wonder and helped people see the wondrous in the ordinary.[5]

"As Augustine most eloquently said, 'God himself has created all that is wonderful in this world, the great miracles as well as the minor marvels I have mentioned, and he has included them in all that unique wonder, the miracle of miracles, the world itself.'"[6] In a sense, such inner experiences are inner icons, painted pictures of the holy that come alive when the Spirit touches us. They are meant to disclose God's love. They are not to be considered dictation from God, but a human way of talking about the way God meets us in daily life. In his Apostolic Exhortation *Verbum Domini*, Pope Benedict XVI referred to such personal experiences and intimations as "a matter of nourishing faith, hope and love."[7] They are meant to be shared and to carry those who hear them into an experience of the Holy Spirit.

Of course, there are false visions. Such visions cause us to hate, isolate ourselves, wear them as badges of holiness, or are against the teachings of the Church. For visions to be helpful, they must be in accord with the teachings of Scripture and should leave us all with a peaceful feeling. They are subjective like our feelings yet rooted in a God who works tenderly in the depths of our humanity.

This doesn't mean that objectivity does not have role. It certainly does. Scripture is objective as well as subjective. The wondrous comes to us not just through visions, not just through spiritual experiences, but by seeing God under the cloak of the ordinary in our regular lives. When creation startles us with its beauty, when the entire world is fresh for us and dancing because of God's love, it is a spiritual experience. Perhaps most importantly, the ways we love each other are ways that God comes to us and through us; God is about relatedness. The Trinity is a dynamic relationship, a dancing, a movement that invites all of us into the flow of love. Some of the early Church Fathers, the Cappadocian Fathers who lived in the fourth century, saw the Trinity as a circle dance. God can also dance in all our hearts and I pray that is what this book leads us toward.

Visions and wondrous experiences do not mean that we are holy. Thomas Aquinas once remarked that if visions meant holiness then we should have to canonize both Balaam and his donkey because his donkey saw the angel and the sword just as Balaam did and was startled (Numbers 22-23). We should also be very careful about taking visions too literally. They are like music, like a painting, not meant so much to give us a manual on life, but to disclose the one life and one love behind all things.

Spiritual Experiences Can Help Rescue our Lives

A while back, I came across the phrase "romancing the jolt" in a book by Sylvia Cary.[8] The concept made its way deep into my heart. We can open ourselves up to the holy through prayer and spiritual practice. By no means are visions badges of holiness. Visions are not even the greatest human experience. They merely offer a tinge of wonder to the ordinary.

When a person cannot help himself, sometimes only a jolt from above can let him know there is a higher power who can help in times of need. There is a story of such a vision in my own family's history. My Uncle Guthrie, my mother's brother, was caught up in alcoholism. He was a hard worker, a very good man, but he couldn't break the chains of alcoholism. It was ruining his family. It was beginning to affect his job. Then, one night he had a very vivid dream: his father-in-law, a Baptist minister who was now deceased, came to him in a very loving but firm way and said, "If you don't stop this alcoholism, you'll die alone." He also said, "God will help you." That started him on the road to recovery.

A Language beyond Words

I experienced visions and wonder at various times in my life when I needed them. Through the wonder of those visions and the hope that was planted in me, I went on to live a fruitful life despite my major physical disability. Part of what I experienced I now call "Messages from Heaven."

Very early in life, I had a vision of healing light, of bright wondrous light. I have had times when I sensed God touching me and speaking in a language of the quiet that has no words, a language that is too deep for words, expressing things that words cannot adequately describe. I often interpret as I write and speak the messages too deep for words, inadequately putting language to something that language can only point toward.

I like to call these experiences what Juliana of Norwich called them—"showings." I find each time I remember a vision vividly, each time I remember a time of "showings," it comes alive for me again, starts over, reruns, and continues as a source of richness. Each time I go back to these wells, there is even fresher water.

I've written these down from time to time for readers. They are an interpretation of an ineffable experience and therefore fall short, but just as the great spiritual writers talked about such things and gave such messages in their own writings, I feel I must write mine. When I read them over, I see new insights. The voice that gave them starts over again and enriches them. Even as I edit and look over the manuscript of this book, they come alive and greater clarity comes. It is like a television program that's recorded and played repeatedly, but each time it's a little different, in greater focus with more depth. It is like an artist attempting to paint a picture he holds in his heart. He paints over and adjusts it many times until he feels it truly represents the image in his or her heart.

I use an old established devotional form of writing in which the first-person voice of God speaks directly and intimately to the reader. Written in vivid, poetic imagery, these words touch not only the surface but the subconscious depths. The language Jesus uses is heart-to-heart. It is as though the reader can feel his warm breath blow over them.

Incorporating first person words from Jesus is a classic Christian genre, a way of sharing intimate devotion. Five hundred years ago, Thomas á Kempis wrote sizable portions of *The Imitation of Christ,* the most enduring Christian classic of all, in this genre. Jesus speaks in first-person voice, both calming and challenging the reader. For instance, Jesus says in *The Imitation,* "That good and sweet feeling which you sometimes experience, is the result of my grace working in you, and is a foretaste of what you will one day enjoy in your heavenly home."[9]

I first read *The Imitation* when I was in college. In those words, I felt Jesus visiting my heart, conveying his love, letting me know that he wanted to speak to me in the silences. One passage in particular meant the world to me. It said, "My son, hear my words, for they are exceptionally sweet and surpass those of the philosophers and wise men of the world. They are to be listened to in silence and received with all humility and deep love. From the beginning I have instructed the prophets, and even now, I do not cease to speak."[10]

Another classic in this genre, from the fourteenth century, is St. Catherine of Siena's major work *The Dialogue of Divine Providence,* a dialogue between a soul who "rises up" to God and God himself. More recent classics that use this style of writing include Thomas Merton's *The Seven Storey Mountain* (1948) and *My Daily Bread* by Fr. Anthony Paone (1954). Merton concludes his book by writing out in God's voice what he felt God was saying to him. Fr. Paone's book of daily meditations includes a "voice of Christ" section and third-person reflection and a prayer. The book highlights that first-person words from Christ is an acceptable genre for Catholic devotional books.

My book, *Letters from Jesus*, was written this way. Some of this book is written that way. This long-established genre leads the reader on a powerful journey into the love of God. This genre can capture afresh the humanity of Jesus as almost no other genre can. Jesus' words can awe, enliven, and knit back together again readers who linger with him as they read the messages. They are a form of heart-to-heart communication with the reader, not lightning from heaven.

These words are a human experience mediated through our humanity, our emotions, and our memories. These are human and earthly touches by God interpreted through my unique personality. Rather than a major supernatural encounter, they are, I pray, signs of the Holy Spirit touching our humanity. Unlike some who write of their spiritual encounters as though they were set off from the rest of human experience, these intimate words for me are part of human experience, yet are real touches by God.

This is a crafted and edited book, but one I pray comes straight from my heart with a touch of the Spirit. I hope and pray that this book calls you to swim in wonder, discovering God in the deep places of your heart.

Chapter One

A Major Disability

The diagnosis was not a good one. It showed significant impairment. Despite the grim words that were conveyed to me, "major neurocognitive impairment," my heart leapt. I now understood a mystery that had haunted me my entire life. Dr. Macintosh said he did not know how I had managed to finish high school, much less complete college and write two books, with the level of impairment I had. I had just undergone several days of neurological and neuropsychological testing to evaluate symptoms that had accompanied me most of my life. The diagnosis also included right-hemisphere brain impairment.

All my life I had been plagued by a puzzling set of problems. Simple basic tasks like putting on clothes and getting ready in the morning were very confusing to me. I would often start them and then catch myself sitting still, paused, not knowing what I was doing. Visual-spatial tasks were confusing. I also had a couple of learning disabilities. My handwriting was nearly completely illegible. Math and science were enormously difficult for me in school. I couldn't remember numbers very well. Keeping anything straight or neat was impossible for me. My room easily turned into one great mess. My condition had created all sorts of problems just with daily existence.

I had gone to one of the premier institutes in America for the study of brain dysfunction and impairment. The diagnosis came from neuropsychologist Dr. William Macintosh of Roosevelt Warm Springs Institute and neurologist Dr. Marcello Estrada, also of Warm Springs Institute.

I Failed at So Many Things

Growing up, my condition had been a great puzzle to me and to those around me because I was so bright with words; I seemed so intelligent. Obviously, the left part of my brain that handles words was working beautifully, but in going along in life, I had failed at so many things. Now this diagnosis gave me an understanding of why.

According to the testing, my verbal IQ, my facility with words was near genius, but my performance IQ, measuring the kinds of things that involve non-verbal issues, issues of daily living, was in the retarded range. I was a contradiction built into a living person.

My impairment had been the source of a great deal of shame throughout my life. Other people had labeled it as laziness. I had heard a thousand times, "Eddie, you'll never make it in life."

I let out a sigh of relief and was beginning to understand, but it would take me years, maybe decades, to fully comprehend the problems that had confronted me since I was a toddler. My diagnosis was followed by two years of outpatient neurocognitive rehabilitation which helped me greatly.

It was easy to understand the causes of my problems. In 1946, I was a foot-first breech birth with the cord wrapped around my neck three times, strangling me. The doctor had to use heavy forceps and I was blue from lack of oxygen. The doctor said if it had taken a few more seconds, I would have been dead. The neuropsychologists also considered the possibility that I suffered from gestational issues. I had grown up awkward and clumsy. I spilled my food all over myself. I needed my parents' help in dressing even when I was a teenager.

But, heaven intervened. From the time I was three or four years old, I began having vivid experiences of God. When I was four, I dreamed a dream so vivid, so real, in which I was caught up into heaven. I could hear the beautiful singing of the angels and was surrounded by the light that was also a love that had existed for all time, the one love that turns the universe. When I was thirteen and my life was in a desperate situation, I had a waking dream of Jesus appearing to me in the midst of light, embracing me and assuring me. At many other times throughout my life, I felt the fire of divine touch. In the following pages, I will share some of these experiences and the messages they contain, not only for me, but for all of us.

Chapter Two

Angels All Around Me

I tasted the richness of God when I was very young. My first memories are wonderful memories, the kinds of memories any toddler should have. I felt happy and loved at that time of my life. Both my parents doted on me and I had a large loving extended family which included my grandparents, Granny and Pop; my aunts and uncles; and my cousins.

From the time I was a small child, I could feel God working in my life. My earliest memories are from the summer in which I turned three on August 24th of that year. My father was an electrician in Columbus, Georgia. His work sent him to school in Philadelphia for a month and he took mother and me with him; we stayed in a hotel while he went to school. Those memories are wonder-filled. I remember the train ride up to Philadelphia. Looking out the window and seeing the buildings and the trees flash by me was utterly fascinating.

Soon after we got to Philadelphia, we took a one-day excursion to New York City. We left early in the morning and took a tour on a bus. We were on the Staten Island Ferry looking at all the big buildings and the Statue of Liberty. In that amazement, I felt God's hand.

Back in Philadelphia, I remember the happiness of having my mother take me to the park every day where I would watch squirrels playing in the trees. The squirrels were the most intriguing creatures I had ever seen. We didn't have big green parks like that in my hometown of Columbus and it was a joy to be in them.

My Father's Baptism

To me, my father was the best father anyone could have. I would wait at the corner for him to come walking back from the mill which was three blocks away. He was an electrician and would get quite dirty, but he always took a shower at work and dressed in a suit coat and tie to walk home. I would wait anxiously for him to come home every day and leapt into his arms.

My parents professed Christian belief. My mother was baptized when she was a child in a Baptist church. Despite this, when I was small we did not go to church. Later in life, I found out that part of the reason for that was that Mother had been raised in a Baptist orphanage. As she put it to me, she had been beaten many times and held a bunch of anger towards organized religion. But, when I was four, my parents started going to a Baptist church with their close friends, Charlie and Mary Harris. My father had a profound experience of encountering Christ and was baptized.

The night of his baptism, Mary Harris took me from the nursery at the back of the Church so that I could see my father's full immersion into the water. During that period, my father became my first teacher of religion. He prayed with me every night, read Scripture with me, and showed me pictures from the Bible. He taught me to pray the Our Father, the Lord's Prayer; the 23rd Psalm; and other prayers.

God became so alive to me. I could feel his presence with every breath. I loved to pray. Even long after my father finished praying with me, I still prayed. I often found the fiery presence of God in my little heart. I sat in the Sunday School room and the teacher showed us beautiful pictures of Jesus. When I looked at them, my young heart was flooded with the warmth of an unspeakable love.

My First Vivid Encounter with Heaven

Daddy had just read me the story of Jacob's dream where he saw angels ascending and descending on a ladder. My father showed me a beautiful, stunning picture in the big family Bible of angels climbing up and climbing down a staircase to heaven. My heart leapt at that image.

I fell asleep later that night and had a dream that was more real than real—vivid, lucid, clear. I dreamed that I was sitting at the bottom of that stairway, watching it all happen. I felt surrounded by love and drank in eternity. This time the angels were not in a picture—they were alive and they were ascending and descending from heaven with a beautiful light shining all around them as heavenly light poured over me. There was a quiet heavenly singing all around that seeped into the very texture of my soul. It was as if I was there and I rejoiced that God was so good.

More than anything, even at four years old, I wanted to be a Baptist minister when I grew up. I would even practice giving sermons in the back yard.

Chapter Three

A Tragic Turn in My Life

Things did not stay so happy and so joyful. My father, as I later learned, had a sudden onset of mental illness when I was five. His new faith had not caused that onset. Rather, as it is with most serious mental illness, it was biochemical tides within his body; it is only now as an adult that I understand that. He turned very hateful. Even at that early age, I was clumsy, messy, and disorganized because of my disability. He would rant at me for not being able to throw a ball right or do other normal things.

At night when he came to pray with me, he would talk about how hot hell was and that there was fire that continued forever that I could not escape from. Then, he talked about the unpardonable sin. I didn't understand what he meant, perhaps it was my clumsiness, but he was inferring that I committed it and that I could not be saved. All of a sudden, my religious world began to crumble. I was headed for hell and no one, not even a minister, could save me.

My father finally became so ill that he started speaking unintelligibly at work and was committed to the hospital for a while. I could not fully work through all of this at that time. I remember being so scared when he was in the hospital.

Also, when he was in one of the delusions, or states as I now know them to be, he threatened to kill me. With an angry hateful look in his eye, he came up to me and poked his finger in my chest and said, "Eddie, if you misbehave, I will cut you here and there." He used his finger to slice up and down my belly and chest. I was terrified. I could not tell anyone else. I was so bad that my father might have to kill me. That was a terror that got planted in my heart.

During Daddy's first episode, my mother was angry with the Church. Our family was financially strained and she thought the Church should help us out. When they didn't, she felt deserted. Her pre-existing rage against Baptists became even stronger.

My father's illness greatly injured my self-image. The one who taught me the wonderful words of our God now told me I was so worthless that if I misbehaved, I deserved to be cut up. That's a lot for a child to deal with and I had no one to explain it to me. It was as though I carried the weight of the world on my shoulders. I did not know how to let the burden I was carrying down.

A Glimmer of Hope

As the years passed by, Daddy's illness came and went. For the most part, he was able to hold a steady, paying job. Some times were better than others. Even though we did not go to Church, these were the days when public schools still taught the Bible. I remember my first-grade teacher reading to us from a children's Bible every day. Other teachers did the same. I was so fascinated with that book. I hoped somehow there might be a secret in that book that would lift the weight of damnation from my shoulders. I felt weighed down and frightened most of the time, but just hearing words from that book gave me some hope. There was part of me that still felt God.

When I learned to read, I started reading the New Testament. I would spend hours in the rocking chair in my room reading the Bible. I still felt that I was probably damned, but I was entranced with the figure of Jesus and with the wonderful pictures that made the stories come alive.

Chapter Four

Precious Memories: Pop and Granny

When things turned tumultuous and scary at home due to my father's illness and my mother's depression, a mountain of shame weighed down on me. A place of solace and comfort was in the presence of my grandparents, Pop and Granny. Both had a Native American background. Pop was half Cherokee, born in the North Carolina mountains. He was also a baptized Baptist and loved God. He was a stronghold fortress for me in my growing up. There were no strings attached to his love, no shame. Though fully Christian, he held to some of the sacred customs of his people.

My grandparents lived in a small white stucco cabin in Georgia that was set right above the bluff of the Chattahoochee River at its highest point; the rocks created waterfalls that the water rushed through. The greenery of the shore and the huge bluff of the other shore were visible, creating one of the most wonderful beautiful places in all of Georgia.

Daddy had to be hospitalized and my mother wanted to be there with him, so my parents sent me to my grandparents while the worst of it was going on. It was my first separation from my parents and I was in a state of confusion about the condition Daddy was in; I did not know what to do.

My grandfather sensed that. The morning after I arrived, he got me up and had me walk with him along the bluff that went along the river. He said a prayer, "Good morning, Grandmother Sun, good morning. I stand in the middle of your sunrise and by the Creator, I am blessed." Saying this prayer out of his Indian tradition, just being with him and hearing that prayer, calmed my soul.

Pop would sit in his chair in the living room of the cabin and go deeply into a profound state of prayer, silent prayer, contemplative prayer. Though he had never heard the word "contemplative," that is the word that describes the way he prayed. He was aware of all that surrounded him. His deep resting in God was obvious to all who were around him. We did not understand the mystery of it at that time. He was attuned, aware of all things around him. He lived in the present moment. He used to walk slowly along the bluff above the river, sometimes dipping down into the woods, looking calmly at everything with a wondrous gaze, taking it all in.

One day, I asked him, "Pop, what are you doing?"

He said, "Eddie, I'm looking at what is in front of me."

"Why," I asked. "Why are you looking at what is in front of you?"

He said, "Because if you look long and hard enough, it will shimmer and you will see the glory."

Sometimes, he would walk along the bluff with a gourd he had filled with stones so that it became a shaker. As he walked along, he would gently shake the gourd. He would sing me lullabies in Cherokee. A cloud of sacredness seemed to surround him most of the time. The whole Native American culture that my grandfather embodied fascinated me. He knew many stories from the old days which he shared with me. I was full of questions and he was full of answers.

My father, when he was doing well in between his episodes, also taught me much about my Native American heritage. Pop's mother, Mary Elizabeth Ensley, was a full-blood Cherokee from North Carolina. When he was a child, she taught my father how to use a sinew to attach stone warheads to canes to make them into arrows. She was also a healer who could cure most anything with the herbs she found in the woods. Daddy would often accompany her as she found her medicine. She helped form my father's heart. My father felt growing up in the modern world was just one step removed from the Stone Age. He shared what he had learned with me.

Chapter Five

The Scriptures Amaze My Soul
When I am Troubled

God comes to us not only in visions and spiritual experiences, but also in Scripture. Scripture can fill our hearts with the wondrous Presence behind Scripture. I learned of the power of Jesus to reach through Scripture from my Aunt Genella and Uncle Guthrie.

When I was little, my Aunt Genella Crittenden played a vital role in shaping my spiritual life. She was a devout Baptist, raised in the parsonage of the Baptist Church in Odem, Georgia where her father was the minister. Her love of Christ and the Scriptures came from deep within her. I have a vivid memory of the summer I was nine, spending two weeks with her and her husband, my Uncle Guthrie.

When I came to them, I was as frightened and stressed-out as a nine-year-old boy could be. My mother was suffering from a stomach condition; her weight had plummeted from her normal 130 pounds to a gaunt 96. I feared losing her. Daddy was in remission from his mental illness for a while. Yet the shame from my mysterious, yet undiagnosed, disability weighed heavily upon me. I felt all of my symptoms, such as being clumsy and awkward and confused, were a profound sin for which I would be tormented forever. Earlier that year I had seen some awful cartoons that depicted God sending children to hell to be terrorized by demons. This deepened my fear of hell. After that, I lived in constant fear that God would send me to hell also.

A short time later, as Uncle Guthrie drove one of my cousins and me through Birmingham on the way to their home in Center Point, we witnessed a man crossing the street being hit by an oncoming car. I still remember the awful sight of the blood gushing from his head as he lay dying on the pavement.

All these disquieting events bore down heavily upon me. I was terrified of my mother dying. I shook inside with the prospect of being sent to hell. Scenes of the man bleeding on the pavement flashed before my eyes, followed by scenes of my dying in the same manner. Like most nine-year-olds, I kept most of this to myself. Finally, one night as I lay in bed, tossing with worry, it became too much for me to handle alone. I had to tell.

Hesitantly, I made my way to Aunt Genella and Uncle Guthrie's bedroom and gently knocked on the door. A sleepy Aunt Genella opened the door, and the words poured out of me, "I'm sure I'm going to hell." I continued with an account of my other fears: my mother dying and my fear of dying violently like the pedestrian I had seen. Aunt Genella lovingly motioned for me to climb onto their bed where I sat nestled securely between them, my back propped up against the backboard with a pillow.

Their voices were full of warmth and comfort. First, they assured me that God loved me and was not sending me to hell. Aunt Genella pulled out their large family Bible, then slowly and tenderly, pausing often, she read passages from Scripture that soothed and comforted. Fifty years later, I still recall those verses.

"Ask, and it will be given you. Search, and you will find. Knock, and the door will be opened for you. For everyone who asks receives, and everyone who searches finds. For everyone who knocks, the door will be opened. Is there anyone among you who, if your child asks for bread, will give a stone? Or if the child asks for a fish, will give a snake? If you then, who are evil, know how to give good gifts to your children, how much more will your Father in heaven give good things to those who ask him!" (Luke 11:9-12)

After reading the passage, Aunt Genella said, "Eddie, by coming in here tonight, you are asking and seeking. Your heavenly Father won't respond by giving you a snake or a stone, or by sending you to hell. Tonight he offers you his comfort and peace." Then she opened her Bible again and began calmly reading one Scripture after another.

Aunt Genella's slow reading of Scripture wove a web of safety around my soul. Through prayer, my stress and worry were greatly lessened. That calming time with Aunt Genella and the Scriptures was like the mountain of transfiguration for me. In the holy light of the Scriptures, my fears diminished and I tasted something of the glory of God. The world seemed different afterward. Later in my life, I discovered that the slow, prayerful way Aunt Genella read Scripture was similar to a traditional way of praying Scripture called *lectio divina*, or "divine reading," which opens our hearts to the embrace of God. The Scriptures can astound us with God's power to relieve our stress and worry.

31

Chapter Six

Jesus Appears to Me and Comforts Me at the Darkest Part of My Childhood

When I turned thirteen, Dad's mental illness, diagnosed as paranoid schizophrenia, turned pernicious again. It also came at a time when my Cherokee grandfather, a devout Christian full of God's presence and a strong presence in my life, was dying of cancer. Pop's illness weighed heavily on me. I shut down my emotions. I could not imagine life without him. He was my connection to a very sacred American Indian heritage, a heritage that would be nearly gone with his death.

He got so sick that he could no longer sit in a chair, and my father had to come over and carry him into the bedroom where he spent the last few weeks of his life. Pop asked me to come into the bedroom with him, but I was too terrified of seeing him sick and dying that I wouldn't enter that room then or in the four weeks he suffered until he died. He asked for me often, but I refused. That later became a burden of guilt on me that only God could help lift.

Daddy was Wild with Paranoia and Rage

Meanwhile, Daddy was wild with his paranoia and rage. His voice sounded threatening. As I thought to myself back then, Daddy talked to me like I was a dog. He was especially upset with me because of my disability. I was going through hell. I remember once my parents and I were driving along a viaduct in Columbus and Daddy looked at my mother and me with his eyes intent, dilated with what seemed like hatred. He threatened our lives and said, "I'm going to get me a gun."

The next day he did show up at the house with a gun. My mother was shut down and depressed. She had no energy and no way of dealing with my father's mental illness. Before things proceeded any further, I got her out of the house. We went to Charlie and Mary Harris's house and from there to Birmingham to be with my Uncle Guthrie and Aunt Genella.

No Escape

My mother, who at times could be a rageaholic, also shamed me about my disability. She shrieked, "If you don't change right now, if you don't change your voice, if you don't change your ways, start acting normal, organize things, and stop being awkward and clumsy, your life's going to be ruined. No doubt about it, you will live a ruined life." There was no escape from my parents.

I could not escape at school, either. Some of my peers made fun of me. One time, I had just picked up an armful load of books from my locker. An older boy came along and knocked them all to the floor. I had to bend down, picking up each book in my arms again while the students gathered around me and laughed. I did not feel like living.

I thought maybe now was the time to end it all. Not only had my father threatened to kill me, I sensed and knew my mother also had deadly intentions. When things were very bad, she broke down and talked to my Aunt Genella about how hard it was to live with Daddy when he was in the throes of his illness. She said, "All I could think about was how to take myself out and, of course, I'd have to take Eddie out with me. That was the hard part." My mother thought causing my death would be better than living with Daddy. I was in mortal danger from both my parents. It was a horrible time, a dreadful time.

Jesus Appears to Me

Numerous ropes of terror encircled my heart and were pulled tight. One day after school, I came home to the empty house. I was full of despair. I put a vinyl record of Beethoven's Pastoral Symphony on the HiFi and as it played, it calmed me down. I felt peace wash over me. My burdens melted away from my heart. As the music played, a gentle, vibrantly alive light surrounded me. The light was all love, all comfort, all tenderness. It surrounded me and filled the room. I could feel myself breathe in the light. It filled every cell of my body with brightness. I asked the light, "Who are you?" and the light said, *I am the one who comforts little boys.*

"I am big," I said. "I am no little boy, but a teenager."

And the light, speaking without words but in a message the heart can hear clearly said, *You are still a little boy, Eddie. I am here to love you, to brighten your heart, to absorb all the dread from every tidbit, from every molecule of your soul and body.* Then it seemed that the light gathered up into a solid person, the person of Jesus. I could see his wounds. I could see the light flow out from those wounds. I could see his love for me written on his face. I could see the brightness where the wounded spots were and heard, *I can illuminate your hurt spots so that they shine with wonder.* Then I felt a sacred hand on my chest and heard the message, *I plant in your heart with love. When the time comes, you will know what to say, but I plant in you a message of love and healing to share with thousands.*

I loved to write despite my terrible, almost nonexistent, handwriting. I would scratch out stories. I dreamed of being a writer when I grew up. I asked, "Will I ever write books?"

The light said, *You will write many books and many hearts will be warmed from the words you write.*

The Lord continued, *I have loved you with an everlasting love. With my love comes wonder and with wonder comes the experience of a world to come: A world that is and a world that will be where diseases are healed, grudges left by the wayside, people reunited in love, creation made new. Have this vision be created deep in your heart for this is your destiny: all things brightened with light, the very light of God. I need you to move onward in your life toward a time when all things will be made whole, all things will be changed. Think of all the love you have felt in your life. That will be returned to you. Think of all the pain and agony you have felt. That will be taken away. Know that Pop, your grandfather, is now with me and he cherishes you and you can see him again one day.*

Chapter Seven

Let Me Show You a Glimpse of Heaven

My disability made it very difficult, if not impossible, for me to play sports when I was young, but that didn't keep me from wanting to play. There was a group of us in the neighborhood that would play backyard sports. The other kids tolerated my awkwardness and clumsiness. I was always the last one picked, but I was always welcome. Even though I never scored and even though it was difficult, they were kind to me, and never made fun of me. They were always there to be my friends and I thoroughly enjoyed taking part in the games.

But when I tried out for Little League Baseball, it was a different story. I attempted several things in the tryouts, but was clumsy and flubbed all the various positions I was supposed to play. I was rejected after failing to catch even one ball. I was deeply embarrassed in front of the coach and everyone else. Not being able to play sports, which I would have loved to have played, was a major source of shame for me.

When I hit junior high, I made a mess of all things that required physical skill. I loved the world of art, including pictures and the art that I found in books. However, due to my disability, my own attempts at creating art with watercolors or pastels came out poorly. I always felt very inadequate.

In the Presence of the Coach, My Disability was Gone

In a recent dream, I was back in school. It's not clear whether it was high school or college or afterwards, but there was a coach and a team, and I played perfectly. I was selected for all the different sports teams: basketball, baseball, and football. I could handle the ball with ease, movement came naturally to me, and I had no motor problems like I do in real life.

The coach followed me around and encouraged me. Then he looked at me and said, "Eddie, you're a beautiful athlete." I felt an enormous grace that I knew to be the grace of God. This coach was enabling me to do things I had never done. In that dream I also hiked up a mountain and drew pictures that were beautiful. I knew that my disability wasn't there anymore. My heart was full of love for others. I knew that the coach was the one who enabled me. Just by being in his presence, things were okay.

It was only upon awakening that I thought I knew the identity of the coach. He was Jesus, not with the long beard and robes, but dressed like a coach in his late 30s. In that dream I saw God's presence saturating the earth, in the very ground beneath my feet. I saw so many different people, and it was so easy to love them all. I still do not fully understand the meaning of this dream. I think it is telling me of a future glory—the new creation, the new Jerusalem—that we are moving toward rapidly. In that glory I will be able to experience all those things I wish I could have experienced while growing up; all the things that, even now, I still miss.

The dream of the coach was followed by a series of dreams of being able to do things that are not in my capacity like hiking up mountains and playing basketball. In those dreams and in the dream of the coach, God was very near—in and around me and through me. All that I saw was a mirror reflecting his image. What I was experiencing was a taste of glory when all things will be made new and whole.

Chapter Eight

Hope Lifts Me Up

The vision I had when I was thirteen in which I saw Jesus in the light gave me some hope but did not change my environment. I still had to deal with Daddy who would come in and out of his illness. My mother could be very hard on me, too, warning me that unless I changed right away, I would live a ruined life. I still was just as clumsy and awkward and had all the visual-spatial challenges I always had. I had so much fear built up inside me. It was consoling to remember when the light came, but nothing in my outward circumstances was hopeful.

After my experience of light, I began to read lots of books by mystics. One of the books that touched me was W. Somerset Maugham's *The Razor's Edge*. Even though it was not from a Christian source, my heart throbbed as I read of one man's search to find the fullness of God. Somehow, I realized that I was on that same search.

Soon after, I discovered the poet T.S. Elliot. It's most unusual for someone that young to be reading T.S. Elliot, but when he spoke of the despair of the modern world, such as in his poem "The Hollow Men," it spoke to my soul of the barrenness of my own life. The soaring Christian poems he wrote after his conversion to Anglo-Catholicism, particularly "Choruses from the Rock" and "Four Quartets," were full of religious and mystical imagery. I read these poems over and over again until I memorized them.

A New Environment

I only passed 9th grade, my last year of junior high, because I went to summer school, but then I went on to the big world of high school at Jordan High School in Columbus, Georgia and my life took a turn for the better. It seemed that high school was a more mature place. I found that the students did not harass me, and it was easier to make friends.

Even though I had almost flunked the 9th grade, my standardized scores on tests of verbal knowledge were extremely high and I was put in advanced classes. My teacher told me there was a new experimental class on creative writing. Margaret Cox, the dean of the school, was head of that class. We shared poems we liked and wrote poems and short stories. She was amazed by the fact that my favorite poet was T.S. Elliot.

She was also the guidance counselor of the 2000 students in the high school. In those days, we never opened up about our problems and I did not tell her anything of my difficulties at home. Her intent was for me to achieve as much as I could with her help. She spent what seemed like hours per month with me. We mostly went over poetry that we liked together and talked about our readings. She was a creative writer and a published author, and we talked about her poems and her work.

She took me aside and said, "Eddie, you are going to write books when you grow up. You are going to accomplish so much." She was saying to me just what the light had said to me in my vision.

My life turned very much for the better and my grades greatly improved. I still had learning disabilities in science and math due to my visual-spatial problems and my handwriting was as messy as ever, but Miss Cox sent out word to all my teachers that they were not to take points off for my messy handwriting, but instead were to carefully read what I wrote and grade on the content.

As I became a teenager, my speech impediment all but went away. Miss Cox and her good friend Helen Shepherd prepared me to do oratorical contests. I won the regional Voice of Democracy contest and the state contest for the Sons of the American Revolution. I began to make real concrete achievements. This helped reduce the shame of my disability.

Daddy's illness was in remission. We had some very positive experiences together and took some fun vacations to Quebec, Williamsburg in Virginia, and other significant places. My relationship with my parents was in much better shape, but I still doubted their love because I had seen what seemed so good turn so perilous so many times.

Plans for the Future

While I had some outward success, a ton of emotional stress still weighed down on me. I still struggled to organize things for my classes in high school. A tremendous amount of fear still gripped my heart from the times that things were not going well as a child and from the terror I had faced. Even though some things were working out, I still felt fearful inside about how I could ever live on my own in the future by myself.

I went with several friends to Edgewood Presbyterian Church in Columbus. The Presbyterian Church had an intellectual Christianity. I thrilled in that and began to fall in love with theology, particularly the theology of Karl Barth, a Swiss Reformed theologian. I felt God pouring out his love into my heart and my heart leapt at the thought of possibly becoming a minister.

I still had the daily struggles of getting dressed in the morning, still had the troubles of organizing anything, but there was lots of hope in my life. What the vision had told me internally was being said by people outside it. I felt a call to share faith with other people. I went off to Belhaven College (now University) to begin my studies toward becoming a Presbyterian minister.

Chapter Nine

I Can Swoop You Up in My Love

As I sat in a chair writing this chapter, wondering what to say, I felt Christ take my hand and I paused and felt the following message form in my heart for my readers.

I heard the sacred voice in my heart saying:

The most important thing I want you to know is my love for you. This is the stupendous good news that underlies the universe. All stars, all galaxies, all light, a beautiful waterfall, the majesty of nearby mountains, a mother caressing the cheek of her infant with her hand, all are my apparel. The whole universe, every particle of creation, comprises my vestments. And if you look hard enough, prayerfully enough, at creation around you, you can grasp some of the infinity of my beauty.

In these messages I am calling you on a journey, a journey into your depth and my depths. Yet all is not right with my world. Sin, discouragement, illness, loss, terror, and loneliness also present themselves. Perhaps you are discouraged. Perhaps hurt grips your heart. Maybe the one you so loved is no longer there to love you back. Perhaps your life appears to have no purpose. You may find that anxiety and nervousness frequently tighten your chest or that you find little hope.

Don't be afraid. In a moment, I can swoop you up into my embrace and you can taste the sweetness of my love, savoring the fullness of my beauty. They are eternity's secret balm and medicine and can be a curative for all discomfort and dissatisfaction.

You will journey to me and with me. As you read these messages, let the sea billows of my eternal care sweep over you. You will swim in wonder.

For the reality is that you have messages within you, too: messages from my Spirit stirring within you; messages from Scripture planted deep inside you. In those messages I say, "Come to me. Let down your load and let eternity erupt from within you. You are very dear to me and I can bind you tenderly to me with cords of love."

As you read the messages in this book, your own messages can be released, for I am always talking to you. Cling to me as the child clings to the parent and I will make all things new and fresh for you.

Through these messages, I am calling you to a deeper love, a deeper knowledge. My love for you is vast, vaster than the universe. My love for you is greater than the greatest oceans. Even the infinity of space cannot describe the lengths and depths of my love for you. I love you in small ways, too. I love you tenderly. As a mother nurses her child, so can my love nurture you. For when you are hurting, I can be right there with you to take your hand, warm your heart and warm your body with the infinity of my caring. My caring is found in the depths of your being, in your heartbeat, in your breath. I am nearer to you than your heartbeat and your breath.

I am with you when you are caught up in destructive patterns, fear, resentment, and isolation. I am there to give you a strong hand to pull you up. When you are facing behaviors and things in your life you cannot change by yourself, you can call to me. I am the higher power who will give you aid when no aid seems possible.

I come to you through my word spoken through the prophets, the Scriptures, and finally in my love made touchable and manifest in Jesus. My love for you is in the breaking of the bread and the drinking of the wine as you taste me. When you are broken, like the Eucharist is broken, know that I can be with you. Just as the host is broken and yet one, so can I heal your brokenness with my brokenness. When you anguish and are in deep despair, if you come to me, I will lift you up. When there seems no pathway ahead, I will make a pathway for you. My love for you is like the Father's love: strong, firm, and gentle with the gentleness that only fathers can feel.

Have you ever felt the burdens of the world weigh so heavily upon you and then finally a friend listens and you're able to break out in song because you know that someone is with you? This is how I love you. I love you in the joyful times, too, for I am a God of dancing and joy. Take delight in me just as you delight in an infant or a sunset or a mountain or an ocean. You can delight in me. My love can even conquer the dread of death. As I was raised from the dead, so can you be raised from that fear of death for yourself and for others.

After a dull winter, spring comes. Shoots of green come up from the earth, flowers blossom, and trees fill out beautifully with green. I am the one who brings springtime to your life. When life becomes bleak and cold, through my presence, through the warmth and enormity of my love, I can bring springtime for you. When you feel most alone, I am nearest to you. Call on me. Call on my name. Touch the cloak of my garment for I will never abandon you. I will never leave you. I will never let you go. Hold onto me.

My love is like a reunion. Reunions can be joyous times. Meeting old classmates, reconnecting with people from your youth, going back to the house you grew up in. When you call on me, you feel the brightness of reunion.

My love is rest. After a prolonged period of exercise, I am the rest that comes when you finish. I am the rest that comes to you after toil and labor. I am the God who helps you after long struggle.

Jesus Offers His Healing and Help

I see a vast plain and Jesus centered there in that vast plain. I see a man going up to Jesus with fear in his eyes, the muscles around the eyes twitching, fear showing in his very bodily stance, and he says to Jesus, "I am addicted to pornography. I can't help myself. I've tried, but I can't help myself. Only you can help me."

And Jesus smiles and says, *I can. I can help you. I can be with you, inside you, to give you strength. When you start to fall, call on me. I can be with you. My help is an incarnational help, rooted in the earth, rooted in nature, rooted in your concrete situation. Go and find others who will help you. Others who have been on the destructive journey you have been on and are turning away from it, toward me, are here to help you, too. For I help you one-on-one, but it is not just a one-on-one relationship you need. You have sisters and brothers and it is through those sisters and brothers that I come. I will help you in your deep interior to break free, but you also need the hand clasp of others. I will guide you all along the way.*

What you seek in pornography is really intimacy, but pornography is a false intimacy. There is no risk of self, no sharing of self, and no ability to endure the pain that it often takes to form a lasting relationship. Seek deep intimacy with me in your heart, in sacraments, and in others. Seek intimacy with others: the special intimacy of husband and wife, the intimacy of spiritual friends, the intimacy of helping and being helped. Look for true intimacy in all its myriad ways and you will no longer need false intimacy.

Seek my love in Scripture. Let the very words of Scripture entrance you. Be pulled into the account of my mighty acts. In those accounts you will find people caught in sin and people delivered from sin and self-destructive behavior. You will see the ebb and flow of my spirit for my spirit breathes in every word of Scripture. Go beyond the surface of the words and you will find me. If you are to know my love, let Scripture be your companion day and night. Enter with your whole self into the words you read for Scripture is my story, but it is also your story. You will discover yourself afresh and discover me afresh when you ponder the words, chewing them like a cow chews its cud.

Another person comes up to Jesus and says, "I am successful. I'm worth several million dollars. I have retired. I've gone to retreats. I've gone to parish missions. I've gone on pilgrimages to the Holy Land and other places, yet I feel dead inside, lifeless and hopeless."

Jesus looks sternly at this man. *If you would feel alive again, touch with your own hands those I would touch: the homeless, the addicted, and the people who just can't seem to make it in life, those that people despise. Let them into your heart and you will let me into your heart.*

Now, in my heart's eye, I see a woman in her late thirties come up to Jesus. Her eyes are red with crying. She says to Jesus, "I lost my thirteen-year-old son to cancer. I not only live with the loss of my son, I live with the agony that he went through on his way to death. No medicine could help him. I could not help him with all my hugs and all my kisses. He went blind well before he died and the screams of his agony still resound within my ears."

Jesus takes his hand, rests it on his chest, then rests his hand on her head and says, *I know agony. I know what it means to scream and have no help. I know what it means to face an immensity of loss. This side of glory, there is no magic pill for getting over such a loss. What I can say is that you can unite your agony with the agony that I felt in my passion, this deep-down agony, and after some time you may see seeds of resurrection come up and bloom.*

Jesus reassures all of us, *My love is with you when you fall into destructive patterns, when you face loss, when you deal with emptiness. I can show you the immensity of my love and gather you up as a mother hen gathers her chicks into the safety of her wings.*

Chapter Ten

A Scary Dream from Heaven

I went off to study at Belhaven College in Jackson, Mississippi to begin my studies toward becoming a Presbyterian minister. The students loved God and the Scriptures. It was an ideal place. No one made fun of me because of my disability. I formed some close friendships. I felt God and I felt the love of my friends. Still something was missing from my life. Just enjoying God and having friends was not enough, but it took a scary dream from heaven for me to learn that spirituality is much more than having good feelings.

The Klan was Burning Churches

Belhaven was an all-white school in the segregated South. Though it later integrated and now has a very open, accepting policy on race, that was not the case when I attended. It was the era of Mississippi Burning, when the Klan burned over forty African-American churches throughout the state, the era when Medgar Evers was murdered. The Klan had infiltrated the Jackson police department and the state government had a special intelligence program to sort out and arrest people that worked for racial equality.

One Thanksgiving, I traveled on the bus to visit my parents in Georgia. The buses were legally integrated at that time, but fear kept African-American people sitting in the back of the bus. I remember being on the bus and looking back into the African-American section where an elderly woman was crying her heart out, sobbing. The bus driver went back to the woman and condescendingly yelled at her and told her not to make such a scene.

Maybe she had suffered a loss. Since I was a ministerial candidate, I thought that maybe I needed to go and comfort her. Instead, fear took over me. If I did that, would they think I was an integrationist, an outside agitator? Would I be beaten up by some of the other passengers? I decided not to act.

A while later when I was back at Belhaven, I had a vivid, scary, spiritual dream. In that dream, I was back on the bus. A thunderclap of an approaching storm sounded. Instead of a woman crying, it was Jesus sitting in her seat, weeping and crying. He spoke these words, "If you don't find me in the back of the bus, you won't find me at all."

I March against the Ku Klux Klan

I knew I had to change. I knew I could no longer stand on the sidelines in the movement toward racial equality. I had to be involved. I got together with Daniel Massey who had similar views to mine. We marched together in a concerted march against the Ku Klux Klan in the streets of Jackson after the Klan had bombed the Jewish synagogue, which had been helping rebuild the burnt churches. They had targeted Rabbi Nussbaum for murder. Luckily, he was not in his office at the time of the blast. Still, there was considerable damage. I remember the fear of walking along that march. Would the Klan show up with shotguns? What was in store for us? At the same time, there was an utter joy in my heart. I was finding out that spirituality was a lot more than good feelings; I was thankful for that dream that had showed me the way.

Never Forget Those who are Desperate

While still in college, I had several dreams about helping the poorest of the poor. In one of those vivid clear dreams, I was standing in a field with Jesus was standing next to me. He had his arm on my shoulder. Some of the people I had loved like Pop and Granny were there as well; I felt their support like my heart was on fire. Then I looked down over a vast immeasurable field and saw hurting people and hurting creation. I saw rabbits wounded by foxes. I saw a kitten with a broken leg. I saw people in great emotional distress. On that plain, I could see vastly. I could see armies warring against one another, killing needlessly, the despair due to the loss of life. The evils we perpetrate on one another were all vivid in a way I cannot fully explain.

Jesus said to me, *Eddie, join with me in the healing.* He kept his arm around my arm and then we raised our hands toward heaven. Healing love poured out from our hearts and from the hearts of many other people who were standing beside us including Pop, Granny, Margaret Cox, and others. We were sending out love to those most in despair, sending out love to a wounded creation. As we sent out that love, healing slowly began to take place. The rabbit that was limping broke free and scurried away. There was a woman who had just lost her only daughter and had no one left to love her whose eyes brightened. So many things happened. I heard this message: *Join with me and let us together heal the woundedness and terror that have afflicted our humanity and our world.*

This message came to me which I knew one day I would share. *When you find me in good friendship and the spiritual sharing among good friends, never forget those who are desperate. Never forget those whose world is being crushed for I send you out as a touchpoint of my love, all of you. You are meant to heal the hurting with love. You are meant to help those who are belittled and discriminated against. You are to help the unborn baby be born into a world of love. You are there because I am there. If you want to find me, you will find me not just in the good times, but in the hurting. Open wide your heart that it may be touched by those who are hurting.*

Chapter Eleven

Christ Reached Out of the Tabernacle and Kissed My Heart with His Presence

After a visit with my parents during spring break, I was on my way back to Belhaven College in Jackson, Mississippi. On that journey, for the first time in my life, out of sheer curiosity, I stepped inside a Catholic Church just off the Highway in Selma, Alabama.

In my part of the South, Catholics were greatly outnumbered. In those days just 2% of the population of my diocese was Catholic. There were grave misunderstandings of those "strange" and "rare" people known as Roman Catholics. My mother was especially anti-Catholic.

I was pleased to be a Presbyterian and had felt no dissatisfaction with the Presbyterian Church. When I stepped inside the Catholic Church, to my surprise it looked very much like a Presbyterian Church. There were, however, a few differences. One was that up front was a gold box with a candle beside it. I didn't know what that box was, but I felt drawn toward it. It was as though God whispered in my ear saying, "Come closer."

I sat down in a pew directly in front of that box. At that moment, love flooded my heart; tenderness, melting compassion, and comfort rose up within me. Warmth coursed through my body. A quiet came over me that was nothing less than the peace of God. Time ceased to exist.

This love was no theological abstraction. Rather it was a great stream pouring through me from God's inmost being; a love that knows no pause. A memory was born that I would relish and draw on the rest of my life.

That moment sent me on a five-year journey that would end with my becoming Catholic. Even though I did not know what a tabernacle was, much less the Blessed Sacrament, Christ reached out of the tabernacle and kissed my heart with his love. It was only later, in talking with a priest, that I learned that box was the tabernacle which contained the Blessed Sacrament.

After that experience, I grew more tenderhearted. It was easier to love others and be sensitive to their needs and feelings. I now knew I had a great reservoir of compassion, God's loving kindness, to help me empathize with those around me. What started as a personal experience of God became one that included relationships with others.

Chapter Twelve

Meeting Mary

During my time in Jackson, my yearning for the Catholic Church grew deeper. I started attending a Catholic Church while I was studying to be a Presbyterian minister, showing up at Saturday night Mass and then waking up bright-eyed and cheery to go to the 11 a.m. service at the Presbyterian Church. I was very conflicted.

I made friends with two Catholic Monsignors who became mentors and yet something still held me back from making the decision to enter the Catholic Church. That was the role of the Virgin Mary. As a Protestant, I had been taught since I was very little that praying to Mary was idolatrous, Mary worship, sinful, and wrong. It is so hard to unlearn such things. I thought as I had been taught: that we can pray to God directly, that we don't need angels and saints, and that we don't need Mary. It was a hard barrier for me to get over, but I had to get over it before I could finally become Catholic.

Would I live my life as a Presbyterian minister or would I become Roman Catholic? My whole life depended on my decision.

One night when I was still in the Presbyterian seminary, I was so distraught that I raised my hands toward heaven and prayed in a loud voice, "Dear Lord, if you want me to become a Catholic, send me a sign." I waited a few minutes and then the phone rang. No, it was not God. No, it was not the Pope. Instead, it was something almost as good.

It was one of my Monsignor friends, who was the head secretary for ecumenism at the national chancellery. He was taking Cardinal Willebrands, a close associate of Pope Paul VI, with him on a tour of several dioceses in the United States. I had been corresponding with the Monsignor about my struggles concerning becoming Catholic, my struggles about Mary, and the weighty decision I had before me. He said to me, "I'm taking Cardinal Willebrands on a tour. We'll be in Austin in three days. I filled him in on your struggles and he would love to talk with you." Talk about a sign. If you can't go to Pope Paul VI, go to his right-hand man.

I met with Cardinal Willebrands and I put it to him bluntly, "How can you Catholics pray to Mary? Isn't that idolatrous? Can't we all go directly to God?"

Cardinal Willebrands, in a firm warm voice, gave me this to think about. "Any Christian day or night can go to God, can talk to God personally one-on-one whenever they want to, but Eddie, don't you also ask your brothers and sisters in Christ to pray for you?"

I said, "Of course I do."

Then he said, "You can ask your brothers and sisters in Christ in heaven to pray for you, too. Because death does not separate the body of Christ, they are a part of us and we are a part of them. We never have to pray alone. We always have brothers and sisters in heaven who can pray with us, and Eddie, who was closer to Jesus than Mary, his mother?"

What he said made an awful lot of sense, but it had to become a matter of my heart. I finally decided to do something spiritually mature. I took a week-long retreat in a Catholic monastery to decide once and for all about Mary and once and for all about entering the Catholic Church. I chose the monastery of Our Lady of Guadalupe Benedictine Abbey in Pecos, New Mexico.

The night I finally arrived there for the retreat, I was tired. But instead of registering and going straight to my room, I went to the chapel. It was empty, but there was a light on, and on one wall I spied a magnificent mural of Our Lady of Guadalupe.

I had never seen Mary pictured as Our Lady of Guadalupe before. It was the most beautiful woman's face I had ever seen. As I looked at it, it seemed that her eyes came alive. In her eyes, I saw an ocean of compassion. Love and delight thrilled me body and soul in her presence. A calm, gentle feminine presence that was the presence of Mary washed through me.

I heard this message from her, *My compassion for you, my children, is greater than all the great oceans, the many oceans, countless oceans. I reflect to you an infinite love from God himself. Find me in tenderness. Find me in compassion. Find me in love of neighbor. I am always there to take your hand, always there to grieve with you if you need to grieve, always there to catch your tears. Just as the angel told Joseph, "Don't be afraid to take Mary home with you," don't be afraid to take me home with you.* I made a firm decision to become Catholic.

Chapter Thirteen

A Message from Mary

As I am writing this, I am sitting before an incredibly beautiful icon of Our Lady of Vladimir, a Russian icon of our wonderful mother. Her features are soft; her robe encompasses her. It is as though the candlelight that surrounds Mary in the painted icon reaches down and encompasses me. She looks tenderly on her son whom she carries in her arms and as I watch it, I hear this message. *I am the mother of all comfort. I can fulfill your deep needs for love and mothering. I have come many times to people to tell them of my son's love. I want you to make peace, peace within yourself, a peace that my hand can help you seal, a peace that my son's wounds can establish.*

If you are filled with anger and resentment, ask me to put my arms around you and pull out that anger and resentment as I embrace you and it will soften you inside. It will calm your passions and leave your heart still, ready to rest in the love of my dear son. I am one who knows how to pray. I am one who knows how to be still. I am one that tenderly looked at my son in his crib, and I can look at you with that same tenderness. I have stood by the cross which healed all those tensions and all those losses, the standing mother, the stabat mater, *giving my son loving looks of support as he was nailed to that tree. In the midst of your trials, I too can give you loving looks of support and take you to my son who was hung on that tree. For his redemption is redemption indeed, redemption that can break the chains of fear and anxiety that might bind you.*

Touch my cloak. In it you will feel the softness of eternity, a time of peace when there has been reconciliation with the warring factions inside ourselves and between us and others. You can let out your disappointments through your tears.

My breath can calm the waves in your soul as surely as my son calmed the waves on the Sea of Galilee. I am human as you are human. I felt the tensions and the losses that this world can give. Light a candle before my picture from time to time and let the light flow back to you from my picture like a shower of love.

Learn to See All as Your Brothers and Sisters

In your world, it is so easy to demonize one another, to look only at the faults, to look only at the bitterness, to make the other non-human, a demon-like creature, because you project onto them your own insecurities. Learn to see all human beings as human beings equally loved by me and my son. They are your brothers and sisters. Never forget that.

It is so easy to feel righteous when we feel strongly that we are right, so easy to condemn others who are not right in the way we are. Learn to see all people as seekers of God like yourself, maybe marred by years of hurt and bitter life but a human like you.

If you harbor bitterness and resentment towards someone, rather than making them a non-person, go to the cross of my son. Look on him who was crucified. As you look on my son and the agony that has healed the human heart and then look on the one you resent, your resentment will fade away. Look on me and you can taste heaven. Look on me and you can taste something more, something more in your heart that you yearn for. I was receptive, docile, yet strong. Learn to be docile, receptive, and strong. I combine tenderness and strength for I am a strong one. I call you to that same docility to the Holy Spirit that I gave in my Annunciation.

I affirmed Mary, "You are indeed the queen of all our hearts. You are glorious, yet so plain and simple and down to earth."

May you always be plain and simple. Resist the urge to feel superior to others. Remember, St. Bernadette of Lourdes was the simplest of the simple and the children at Fatima were just children. Become a child before me, all you who listen to this. Become like a child before my son, eager to absorb the holy presence before the light.

Take Time to Pray

Listen to his whispers in your heart. Take time each day to pray, to sit before the great silence and let the tenderness of all angels and all saints, the brilliance and glory of all saints and all angels, surround you. I call you on a journey, a deeper journey into God's love for there are depths you have yet to plumb. When you go on that journey further and further into God's love, your personality will change. You will grow strong, and yet at the same time, your personality will soften.

Your eyes, your face, will embody the deep rest of heaven. Just by being around you, people will know my presence. Just walking on a street or walking in a mall, strangers will sense something and come up and unburden themselves to you. Listen with great love when they do this.

Pray the rosary. Even the smallest child can touch the rosary and touch me and my son. Yet, even the most advanced contemplatives can use the rosary as a highway deep into the heart of God. Do not look on the rosary as old fashioned or out of date. It has made thousands into saints. Finger the beads with your hand and know you are fingering a lifeline from heaven. There is always more to God, always more to heaven than we dare think, and simple prayer can penetrate into rich glories of eternity.

Chapter Fourteen

Sounds of Wonder

I graduated from Belhaven and went off to Union Presbyterian Theological Seminary in Richmond, Virginia, which was a very different experience. We had to write scores of papers my first year, and I didn't have the warm companionship I had in college. My room was messy. Taking care of clothes was a tremendously confusing task for me—cleaning them, hanging them up, and selecting them. Plus, I felt so alone. We had one of the best faculties of any seminary in the United States and all my professors were kind and good and believed in me, but the depression that came from fear and the anxiety were still with me.

My spiritual experiencing seemed to calm down during this period. I had few visions or spiritual experiences. I mostly felt dry inside. In hopes of finding a better situation, I transferred to Austin Presbyterian Theological Seminary in Austin, Texas for my last two years of seminary. The workload was so heavy that I could not handle it because of my disability. The faculty was not as supportive as they had been in Richmond. I was terrified of not being able to complete my coursework. Also, as my neuropsychological examiners described after testing me for brain dysfunction, I get stuck and phase out at certain points when I have to handle several visual-spatial tasks at a time. Because of my right-brain dysfunction, I would often space out lots of times as I was trying to get ready for class. My appearance began to suffer. I felt so ashamed and so afraid.

Making friends also seemed very difficult. One of the reasons is that people who grow up with visual-spatial problems or nonverbal learning disabilities cannot read the facial expressions or the body language of others. They can't catch the jokes or the subtleties in communication. This makes personal relationships harder for me.

In those days, seminary students could supplement their income by preaching on weekends at churches around Texas. One time I went to a church in central Texas and spent the night in a motel after delivering a sermon. I was depressed. I felt hopeless. I felt caged. There was no way for me out of the situation. I felt no door out of my prison. I despaired of ever having close warm friendships and relationships. I despaired of being able to finish the program. My spiritual experiencing had nearly ceased, so even this source of hope was missing.

In desperation that night at the motel, I started pouring out my soul out loud to God, "Lord, without you I do not know what to do. The landscape around me seems to be dry and barren—a wasteland. I'm unable by myself to change anything. I don't even know how to pray to you, Lord."

Then I opened the Bible and read the passage in Romans where it says despair prays for us with unutterable sighs.

"We know that the whole creation has been groaning in

labor pains until now; and not only the creation, but we ourselves, who have the first fruits of the Spirit, groan inwardly while we wait for adoption, the redemption of our bodies. Likewise the Spirit helps us in our weakness; for we do not know how to pray as we ought, but that very Spirit intercedes with sighs too deep for words." (Rom 8:22-23, 26)

I then turned to St. Paul's Second Letter to the Corinthians, "For in this tent we groan, longing to be clothed with our heavenly dwelling." (2 Cor 5:2) I let my sighs and groans out. No one was there to hear me. The groans turned into a beautiful melody, and I sang that melody without words. I wondered if this was what they called speaking in tongues.

One of my professors who was friendly and supportive was Dr. J. Rodman Williams, who would go on to become a famous theologian. He was involved in the late 1960s and early 1970s with what was known as the Charismatic Renewal which brought back reverence for the Holy Spirit and certain gifts such as tongues, prophecy, and visions. After I got back to the dorm that Sunday night after preaching, I went to a weekly prayer meeting in his living room for people from all over the area. Everyone greeted me warmly. I asked about my experience and they prayed for me for a release of the Holy Spirit. I heard others singing in melodies without words. Those were indeed songs of wonder, beautifully enunciated. Something changed in my life in a mighty way. I felt the inrushing of the Holy Spirit. My own journey was lit up by the experience of the prayer group.

Chapter Fifteen

Living Flame of Love

After my deepening experience of the Holy Spirit, I began to have many visions and religious experiences. God seemed so close. I could fall asleep and find myself floating in his love. He cradled me in a way that cannot be described or put into words. It is as though I floated, and his hands and everlasting arms held me up. This experience of God was so good, but I needed more. There was something deeper that had been tapped in me during my life that I needed to continue probing. I discovered books on contemplative prayer, particularly Thomas Merton's *Contemplative Prayer,* the *Living Flame of Love* by St. John of the Cross, and several books of St. Francis including *The Little Flowers of St. Francis.* In those books I saw people having religious experiences like what I had growing up. Most of these readings came from the monastic tradition of the Catholic Church.

During this time, I also began to form close friendships. One was with Bill Wise who was a student from Saint Edward University, the Catholic school in Austin. He came to Professor Williams' prayer meeting with a large contingent of students from the Catholic college and he and I became fast friends. He possessed a spiritual depth, warmth, and a comforting presence. Unfortunately, he lived on the other side of town and couldn't help me with my clothes or papers like the students at Belhaven had done.

One friend of Dr. Williams was Dick Pickens, a Presbyterian minister who was a real champion of God. He started a Christian living situation and ministry called The Well that ministered to the street people in Austin. They took over an old frat house and I moved from the seminary to there.

A Time of Delight in God

It had an attic that was surrounded with windows that were opened to the cool night. It was deserted during the night and I would go up there to pray. I would pray in what I call jubilation because that's what it was called for a major part of Church history. I would also engage in the Jesus Prayer and would go deeper and deeper saying the name of Jesus in the stillness. There were many visions that came to me during that time. I just felt so much love from God in those prayer times up in the attic. At times I heard beautiful heavenly music. Other times it was as if my heart would beat out of my chest because of the fire of love that I experienced. I fell deeply in love with God.

My long prayer times were a time of delight in which I

sensed God caress my heart. Love poured into me and love poured out of me back toward him. I had a deep growing certainty that I would write books and preach and share the love of God with thousands. I had a great desire to do this despite all the failure in my outward life. It was a perplexing situation.

One day when I woke up, I had a keen sense that something utterly dynamic was going to happen that day. Something was coming. Something was grasping me, and I would never be the same. That feeling persisted. It came like a tingling all over as the day progressed.

Caught up in a Tremendous Love

The door of The Well was always open to those who needed help. Once a week it was my turn to man the door with one other person in order to open the door to anyone who came there during the night. On one such night shift after it was very late and unlikely that anyone would show up, I fell into the couch that would be my bed in the downstairs room. I prayed my Jesus prayer using a rosary ring to reinforce it. "Jesus, Lord Jesus. Jesus, Lord Jesus," I prayed repeatedly. My whole body began to vibrate. Then, in a way I can't explain, I was caught up in the tremendous love — an enormous, tremendous life-changing love that delighted me, sang to me, and softened my heart. Suddenly, I was in a vortex of light and flame. The light was the love of God. With me were millions of others caught up in the light. We were all going through time, all changing, and we were helping those behind and those ahead of us to grow closer to that love. The brightness shattered any darkness. I heard angels singing. Divine sweetness filled me through and through.

The fire of the vortex, the light of the vortex, the flame of the vortex was cleansing: cleansing out impurities, cleansing out doubt and worry, helping me proceed step by step closer to God. The love that I felt was like no other love that I had ever felt before, greater than the love that my mother showed me before things in my family turned disastrous, greater than the love my father showed me before his illness set in, greater than the love of my many friends, greater than the love of Margaret Cox.

The fire and the light conveyed the presence of God, but they were also cleansing inside. It was as though there was an immense amount of love that I felt in every cell of my body. Every cell of my body tingled from the immensity of the love that I felt. There was also pain, pain that needed much cleansing. There were so many messages given to me that night in the language without words. I'm going to strive and try now to put into words some of the things I received that night.

I am an Immensity of Love

One of the main things that I received is this: There is always so much more of the presence of God than we dare imagine. Our imaginations fall short when it comes to God. I heard the fire and light speaking, giving me this message for everyone, not just for me.

I am an immensity of love. You will know me and day by day you can know me more throughout all eternity, but you will never exhaust the beauty of my nearness, the beauty of my presence. I send you out to be a touch point of that presence, to keep telling people that there is always so much more and that when we enter the light of God's presence, we do not enter in alone. We enter in with brothers and sisters and all creation.

In creation, you see my footprints. The fire of my love knits your hearts together, binding your hearts to one another as they are also bound to my heart. There is so much more available to you if you bathe yourself and immerse yourself in the light of my presence. I can change the way you speak. I can help you glow with a warmth that is both human and divine.

You may feel unworthy of my presence, that you are too weighed down with the mistakes you made in life, with the ways you've closed yourself off to me and others. Know that my love forgives all sin, pardons all error. You do not have to be some athlete training hours a day for a marathon. You do not have to make yourself worthy of my presence. You are my child. I am here to forgive as only a parent can forgive, to throw my arms around you and tell you that it will be okay forever.

In times past, people saw my presence. They prayed long hours. They opened themselves up to my touch, and when they did that, marvelous things happened—a whole culture was transformed. Your culture can be transformed, too, for the Church and society are desperate for presence, a touch that lets them taste of God as surely as in the here and now you can taste honey. Taste me, smell me, feel me, breathe me in, and then when you meet people, they will sense the presence of God mediated through you despite your errors, despite your problems. They can be transformed.

Put your Hand in my Wounded Hand

You touch me bodily not only in the Eucharist but in 'the least of these, my brothers,' the disenfranchised, the rejected, those experiencing dark loneliness who have no one to turn to. Find these people. Touch them with your broken humanity and my powerful dynamic presence will heal the brokenness. In the light of my resurrection when I appeared to the disciples, my whole body gave forth light and the parts that lit and shined the most were my wounds. If you wish to touch my wounds, touch the brokenhearted. If you wish for your own wounds to be transfigured so those wounds convey light and hope and the eternity of my presence, touch my wounds.

My love is like warmth. It is like a taste of honey. It is also found in the musicality of creation that can vibrate your whole being. My love is like touch, a mother's touch on her new infant's hand. That is how I touch you. Please let me touch you that way. I can invade you with a love that is everlasting. Open your heart to receive that love. Open your heart by reading Scriptures. Open your heart by extended periods in prayer. Open your heart by spiritual reading. Open your heart by loving others and forming loving bonds of friendship. Open your heart by really touching creation and know that in the beauty of all that is created, you can feel the creator.

You can open up to my love by letting your heart be broken by the hurt of the world. Do not numb yourself to pain, either your own pain, or the pain of others, or the pain of my suffering creation. Grieve. Let the pain flow through you in tears. Tears are a gift, the gift of my love. When you can weep for the hurting ones, you have passed from death to life. Let that feeling of brokenness flow to become an infinite compassion. I am infinitely compassionate and I call on you to also be compassionate. Do not be quick to judge for you do not know all the circumstances of the other person's life. Hold and rein in your judgment. Reach out in love as the Samaritan did to the beaten man.

Look for Me in My Disguises

I heard this message reverberate throughout my being as I was encircled by the fiery being of love:

I have loved you with an everlasting love. You are needed and tied together with all creation, with all your fellow humans. Help one another. You are not saved alone. You are not healed alone. You are saved and healed together with your brothers and sisters forever and always. Your journey is not a lonely journey, but a journey with brothers and sisters, a journey in which you are connected to the one source and fountainhead of love, my love for you.

The more you give away, the more you receive. The more you spend yourself in love of others, the more vibrant my love floods within you. When you touch your brother or sister, you touch me. When your heart knits together with them, your heart is knit with me.

Remember that I come in disguises. I come disguised as the poor and hopeless. I come disguised as one who seems to be loved by no one. I come disguised as the beggar, as the street person, as a child lonely and terrified during warfare. I come disguised as your neighbor who is so hard to love. These are just some of my disguises. Look for me in my disguises.

My people, I yearn for you as a mother yearns for a lost child. I yearn for you as a refugee that yearns for his homeland. I yearn for you in the way a beloved yearns for the beloved. My love is the source of all love. Take the sum of all the loves you have experienced. My love is infinitely greater. You can only experience a little of my love, for you are not ready to see face-to-face. But even though you do not see face-to-face, you still see. Take my hand and walk with me, for I will lead you in the path that you will travel.

Jesus Gives Me Hope

Eddie, you are broken and because of your brokenness, I can use you. Continue to saturate yourself in my presence. You will write the books you always wanted to write, and you will touch many people.

"But how?" I asked the presence. "I'm failing at everything I do. I flunked out of seminary. I can't keep up with my chores and clothes where I live. How?"

Just trust in me, Eddie. I will work out the how. Just put your hand in my wounded hand and things will unfold. There are many things on the horizon you cannot see now. You are broken, even shattered, but bathe your broken and shattered self in my presence and your very brokenness can become a conduit of my love. I know you see no evidence of what will come, but it will eventually manifest itself.

Your relationship with me is not just a personal thing. It involves those who teach you, those who minister to you, those whose embrace is my embrace. It includes all those you will teach and all those you will speak to, for you will speak to thousands of people and talk about this love. I call you to send out this message that we should all be caught up in this love. We should spend our lives with this love, give away all that we have with this love, change our lives so that we follow the yearnings of this love. My love will always refresh you. My love will give you joy.

I saw a high mountain and then heard the message, *Climb to the mountaintop to be with me. I am like the beauty of majestic mountains. Do not be afraid of the heights. Just as I am close to you now, there will be times when I seemingly withdraw my presence so that you may seek me harder and love me more and leave behind you any destructive patterns that have bound you up.*

I saw a picture of my parents with lights surrounding them and I heard the words, *Eddie, I love these two people and they love you enormously. They may have made mistakes in the ways they tried to show that love, but do honor your mother and father because so much of what you will become rests on what they gave you, imperfect though it was. My love came through them.*

The vision was finally over. I do not know if it was a dream. It did not feel like a dream. It felt more real than real and I was caught up in it for the whole night, tingling and experiencing the fiery love and light of God. I knew I had experienced the living flame of God's love, the living flame that St. John of the Cross had spoke of in his book *The Living Flame of Love* which I had read a couple of weeks earlier.

Back to Daily Life

In the following days after these spiritual encounters, life seemed just as hard as it always had been. I kept failing and falling short because of my disability. The call that the light and fire conveyed to me seemed so different from my everyday existence. Only time would see the unfolding of what the fire and light were telling me.

God's presence was thick in my life yet my future was dim. I felt it hard to keep up with the tasks of being in that living situation at The Well. Naturally, I had to help with the tasks of washing the floors, with vacuuming, with keeping things straight—all things that were nearly impossible for me due to my yet undiagnosed neurocognitive deficits.

During this time my yearning towards the Catholic Church grew even stronger. I found that the Church Fathers and the stories such as those I found in early Franciscan literature spoke to my heart. I longed to partake of the

Eucharist. I went to Mass daily at the Catholic student center in Austin. Dick Berg, a psychologist at St. Edward's, went to the prayer meetings that were now held at The Well, and he and I became good friends. He became yet another mentor. Yet, except for my friendships, I was failing at everything I did. Still, I had an inner reassurance that I had a purpose, and all would be well.

Chapter Sixteen

The Miracle of the First Book
I Wrote

One of the things my mother had said to me over the phone when I was still at The Well in Austin cut me to the quick. She said, "Sometimes a mother has such high hopes for her child, then they are all shattered. Eddie, you have shattered my hope in you." That weighed heavily on me. I knew I couldn't easily do things in the physical realm and I didn't know why. I was asked to leave the seminary because of my academic record. I did not know what the future held for me. All I had to hold onto were the Scriptures, the Catholic Church which I now belonged to, and these mysterious holy visitations of light and warmth. I returned home from Austin because there was no place else to go.

Though my parents didn't warmly receive me, they did receive me. They thought home was a place you could always go to, no matter what. They didn't understand why I had such a tough time with life. I didn't understand either. Their disappointment dragged on my soul like a ton of weights.

"Why, O Lord, can't I do things like everyone else? I feel so lazy, so shiftless. To use my mother's words, 'so sleazy,' that I can't keep up my appearance. Am I that weak-willed? Am I that sinful? Why, Lord, Why?" The anguished words came from my mouth.

The warmth within me, the light that surrounded me, said, *One day, Eddie, you will understand and know, but for now, just trust in me. I am calling you to write an important book that will change people's whole understanding of faith and the history of my people. Prepare yourself for this book you will be writing. Prepare yourself to speak because you will speak to hundreds of thousands of people and I will guide you each step of the way.*

I then stopped arguing with the light and the warmth. "Your will be done, O Lord. Your will be done. Help me to do your will."

Jesus Leads Me

In outward appearances, it seemed that everything had fallen apart for me. I was overwhelmed by my disability. Just getting through a day was an ordeal. One day, I sat down with my back toward the wall and began saying the Jesus prayer. I felt a light surround me, not as vividly with my eyes open as I did when I was a little boy, but I sensed the light on my skin, in my heart, and all around me with my eyes closed, shining down on me. I said, "O Lord, You keep putting this desire to write a book in my heart, yet everything is so confusing and difficult."

And then, in my heart, I heard this message, *Know that I am the one leading you, Eddie. I am the one who has your hand and guides you through the obstacles. If you were blind, you would need someone to guide you. Your world right now seems like chaos, but I am the one who can lead you through it. Don't doubt that I have called you to write and to speak. I am putting a warmth in your heart right now that will let you know that I will stand beside you.*

"O Lord," I prayed, "my parents are so upset with me. They help me out financially to go to seminary and it's all falling apart. I know that I can't hold any sort of regular job and I don't know why. I just can't do things."

Just take my hand, the Lord said again, and I felt his hand entwined with mine. *By this hand, I will lead you. Please follow my leading. Go ahead and prepare to write your first book. I will be with you. I will show you amazing things. Your book will be published and you will speak to thousands of people.*

This all felt so right and so true and believable. As the Lord held my hand, I was bathed inside by a warm light that came from the warmth and the light of Jesus' own heart.

Soon, I knew what I would be writing about. I had loved the early Franciscan literature, particularly the *Little Flowers of St. Francis* that described Francis' simple humble prayer and how God used him despite his inadequacies. It showed the early Franciscans as a warm community, a warm family. They also had visions, saw signs and wonder, as in the current-day charismatic renewal. This was true not only for saints, but the ordinary people who were part of this community. There were references to jubilation, *jubilatio*, the Latin word for yodeling or singing-crying, that is so much like the speaking in tongues of the charismatic movement today.

Yet, it seemed ridiculous that a young man who had flunked out of graduate school in theology could attempt to write a theological book and get it published. "Who would publish such a book?" I asked myself, but I had an urgency inside me to write that book, an urgency I believed was given by God.

As I prayed one day, the warmth and the light came to me again. *This is not limited to Francis, Augustine and others. Go through the personal letters, the biographies, the autobiographies of people of faith and you will find hundreds of similar instances. This is all waiting for you to discover, but you will have to be the one to find it. I will guide you, I will warm you, I will comfort you, but I am giving you a calling. Show that wonders, visions, and jubilation were at the very heart of the Church for so much of its existence.*

Examples of Jubilation

I began to do research at Auburn University about an hour from my house. There I found amazing things. A whole tapestry of connections unfolded. This jubilation, which the Church taught others and the great mystics and saints prayed with, was widespread. In congregations, it was described as wordless singing on vowel sounds that could go on for a long time. Wondrous things like miracles and healings were associated with jubilation. There were scores, if not hundreds, of quotes in the tradition.

Take, for instance, Thomas Aquinas. Bernard Gui, his first biographer, describes Aquinas praying in this manner when he was at Mass. He "was utterly absorbed in the mystery, and his face ran with tears." Thomas struggled in prayer while he was writing theology. Gui writes, "He never set himself to study or argue a point, or lecture or write or dictate without first having recourse inwardly—but with tears—to prayer for the understanding."[11]

St. Thomas Aquinas himself describes this jubilation this way:

First, (praying aloud) is a way in which we can stir ourselves with our words to pray with devotion. Secondly, praying aloud can keep our attention from wandering, because we can concentrate better if we support our feelings with words when we pray…when our mind is kindled by devotion as we pray, we break out spontaneously into weeping and sighing and cries of jubilation and other such noises…we have to serve the God to whom we offer reverence in prayer not only with our minds, but also with our bodies.[12]

Gui describes a scene when Thomas was teaching in Paris on Paul's writings and came to a difficult passage to interpret. He ordered his secretaries out of the room, "fell to the ground and prayed with tears, then what he desired was given him and it all became clear."[13] Such a catharsis, letting emotions out through jubilation, tears and fervent prayer and cries, attuned him to the spiritual world, and at times visions guided him in his groundbreaking teaching.

With the exception of the New Testament, St. Augustine of Hippo influenced the Church more than anyone else during the first millennium. He mentions jubilation a number of times, especially in his *Commentary on Psalms*. He writes, "Where speech does not suffice…they break into singing on vowel sounds, that through this means the feeling of the soul may be expressed, words failing to explain the heart's conceptions. Therefore, if they jubilate from earthly exhilaration, should we not sing the jubilation out of heavenly joy, (singing) what words cannot express."[14]

Before, everyone had thought that glossolalia, or speaking in tongues, ended with the apostles, but I found these quotes and I felt the urge to research further. I felt there was something major here. We were ignoring a whole part of our tradition and what was in that tradition was earthshaking.

I began to study the enormity of this tradition.

I wondered why none of this was well-known. Then, I thought about how theologians all too often turn to the intellectual side of the great thinkers of the Church rather than the human and ordinary. So, we hear about Thomas Aquinas and his theology and his use of Aristotelian philosophy, but we fail to even look at or pay any attention to the sources that describe him weeping during his prayer, searching with sighs and groans in jubilation for inspiration for his writings.

Miracles Begin to Happen

Early in that period, I paid a brief visit to the Word of God Community in Ann Arbor, Michigan. I wrote up six or seven little summaries of the research I was doing and I asked someone to pass it on to Ralph Martin, the editor of *New Covenant*, one of the most popular Catholic magazines of the time. Much to my surprise, he called me and said, "Come in right away to my office." He continued, "We would like for you to do a series of six articles for *New Covenant* on your research." I was going to be published and have a series in a magazine. This was an amazing thing. Published! I began to trust what the warmth and the light said to me.

I researched further, then I got some help from a community of people where I worked in Allentown, Pennsylvania for a year and a half doing retreat work. I got lots of secretarial help. Without that, it would have been impossible for me to write the book with my disability. Everything came together. I sent the manuscript off to Paulist Press, hoping that I would hear from them, but I was also being realistic. The odds were not in my favor.

It took them nine months before they got back to me. During that time, I despaired of it ever being published, yet the Holy Spirit inside me kept telling me, "Have hope." Then I got a response from Bob Heller at Paulist who said, "Everyone has approved your book. We sent it out to theologians to have it checked. We think we're going to publish it. It just needs to go through the committee." A few days later, I got a letter saying the book had been accepted. Paulist Press is one of the most prestigious Catholic publishers, especially when it comes to publishing theology. I could see this as nothing less than a miracle. They told me that one of the theologians who had reviewed the book before they decided to publish it said it was the equivalent of two doctoral dissertations.

Mary Healy STD, Associate Professor of Sacred Scripture at Sacred Heart Major Seminary, Series Editor for Catholic Commentary on Sacred Scripture, who later read the book, *Sounds of Wonder*, commented on it:

> In this remarkable book Eddie Ensley opens up a whole new window into Catholic spirituality of the last two millennia. Ensley shows convincingly that the gift of tongues and other charismatic phenomena did not disappear from Christian tradition but continued in every age, especially in the form of jubilation, an exuberant prayer of the heart that overflows in wordless vocal praise. This book is a great resource for everyone interested in the charismatic dimension of the Church, which was, as John Paul II said, rediscovered at Vatican Council II.

85

DEACON EDDIE ENSLEY

Chapter Seventeen

A Ministry is Born

Once I knew my book *Sounds of Wonder* was going to be published, I had a real yearning to speak with people about the love and the wonder of God. I felt compelled. It was something that I did not fully understand, but I felt compelled to do that. There was a hunger in me to pour out to people how loving God is and how close heaven is to all of us. At that time, summer and fall of 1977, I began praying with some young men and women of our parish on a weekly basis. We thought we might form a religious order one day; we weren't sure.

One of the young men that met with us was Robert Herrmann. I had first met him at our parish prayer group and I could tell that he was deeply into prayer, especially into the silences. He had about him the softened facial expressions of someone who was God-filled even though he was only twenty years old. We started praying together once every week, just the two of us. We sensed that God was calling the two of us to something. We were not sure what. Our hearts touched when we prayed, very much the way my heart had been touched just by meeting Margaret Cox, the guidance counselor, when I was in high school. We both had an interior sense that God was calling us to something momentous. Robert had discovered contemplative prayer, the prayer of silences, on his own and had special experiences of God coming to him, full of mystery and wonder, infusing his heart with the rich silences of heaven.

One day, we prayed together on the masonry staircase in front of a door after hours. We prayed as we normally did—a little conversational prayer then entering the silences. As soon as I started praying, I felt what must have been a powerful wind sweeping over both of us even though the day was calm. I had imagery burst out of me, showing scenes of us speaking to thousands of people and people being touched. From the look on his face, I could tell that Robert had much of the same experience I did. When we unpacked what happened in the silences with each other, we discovered that we both felt the wind of the Holy Spirit and had visions of speaking in front of thousands of people. It's one thing to have a vision; it's another thing to make a dream like that reality. We had a real sense that we should leave the doing up to God.

We took our interest in starting a ministry to our pastor and to our good friend Father Tom Francis at the Cistercian Trappist Monastery in Conyers, Georgia where we would go to make retreats and for spiritual direction. This great man of God who had about himself a holy foolishness said to make a start and talk to our bishop. We did that next. To our surprise, the bishop didn't say a phrase like, "Come to reality." He said, "I see you both called to something genuine and I can't make things like this happen, but I can shepherd them once they start. You have my blessing."

The Ministry Begins

And so, we started. I had gotten a lot of notoriety in the Church because of my book being sold everywhere and I sent some notices to retreat houses and renewal groups throughout the country telling them we were ready to speak. The invitations started pouring in. The ministry was launched that has since reached about 600,000 people.

I had been invited by a ministry of the Archdiocese of Los Angeles in March 1978 to put on evening retreats throughout the diocese. On this engagement, I went by myself. Many hundreds of people showed up. Some of them had tears in their eyes. We talked about contemplative prayer, about the rich and deep loving ways of knowing God that the Scriptures and our Church give to us. I left them a recording of Robert Herrmann telling about his contemplative prayer life at age twenty. They were so enchanted by it, they invited not only me, but also Robert, to give a retreat to priests and religious of the archdiocese. My heart leapt as I saw Robert read from his spiritual journal to those assembled.

One highlight for us was a period in the 1990s when we were invited up to Canada several times to give retreats on Native Reservations. It was an immense joy for me to be among my own people, talking about the goodness of the Great Creator, Great Spirit; or as we call him in Cherokee: Edota, Father.

Other books came, perhaps most notably *Prayers that Heal our Emotions*, a book that was published by Harper Collins and became a religious bestseller. All told, including this one, I have written fourteen books. Robert wrote one book of his own, *Writing to Be Whole: A Healing Journal*.

Another Call from God

We were close to the Church, but we wanted an even closer connection. We prayed about this and took it to our bishop who was Most Rev. J. Kevin Boland. Before being named bishop, he had been pastor of our parish for many years and we knew him well. He invited us to the seat of our diocese in Savannah to spend several hours with him praying and discerning about our ministry. Nothing was decided at the meeting.

Then, one Saturday I got a call from the Bishop and he said, "Eddie, I think your being deacons, ordained clergymen, would greatly enhance your ministry. I would like for the two of you to consider joining our deacon formation program." We did and four-and-a-half years later we were ordained as clergymen in the Diocese of Savannah.

Our ordination did give us entrance as clergy to preach at parishes on weekends and then to give parish missions. Our ministry, Deacons in Ministry, was later given status as an official Catholic organization, approved by both our diocese and the United States Conference of Catholic Bishops and included in the Kennedy Directory of official Catholic organizations.

Just since we were ordained in 2001, I estimate that we have spoken to over 400,000 people in the Masses we preach for Parish Missions, called Parish Retreats. One special retreat was given at a primarily American Indian Catholic Church in Tahlequah, the capital of the Cherokee nation.

Also, the opportunity came for me to teach in the graduate program for Pontifical College Josephinum.

Though we have struggled financially, our ministry has been a spiritually enriching experience, and I hope and pray that many have been helped and touched.

Chapter Eighteen

Jesus Through
American Indian Eyes

One of the beautiful things I found in Catholicism was that the Church believes in inculturation. This means the Church spread the message of God's love using the symbols of particular cultures. This is especially a good thing for me as a Native American. Saint John Paul II met with 10,000 Native Americans in Phoenix, Arizona in 1987. A native medicine man and third-generation Catholic led the pope through a blessing ceremony. He also went through several healing ceremonies. John Paul II encouraged Native Americans to keep the cultural ways as long as they were in accord with Christ.[15] This greatly encouraged me to include my culture in my spiritual journey, the culture I learned from my father and my grandfather who were both Native American and baptized Christians.

The Sweat Lodge

One expression of that culture is the sweat lodge, a heated hut with a pit in the center for hot stones. At nighttime a fire would be lit and stones put in fire. We would gather in a circle around the stones in the pits, say prayers together, and smoke a pipe that symbolized peace. My native friends Jerome Carter and Claire Inness held a sweat lodge every month or so on their land in Standing Rock, Alabama, about an hour and a half from my home in Columbus, Georgia. It was for people of Native American descent but some other seekers also joined us. All day long participants helped to build the lodge. Due to my disability, I couldn't help build, but I sat and engaged in conversation while the sweat lodge was constructed. We all shared the joys and sorrows of our lives since we were last together.

At night, when the stones were hot, we gathered in a circle. We all sweated, sweating out the toxins of our body while the Holy Spirit was cleansing us from within. It is a profound way of praying, penitential and yet joyful at the same time. As I sat with my bare legs against the earthen floor, I thought of God's gift of the earth that sustained me and how it reminded me of His sustaining love and sustaining power. I came from this earth. I would return to this earth. Yet, I also came from the mystery that envelops this earth in God's embrace as lover of the beloved. Some people would pour water on the stones and steam would blast the whole lodge full of steam. It reminded me of incense in church and prayers lifting to God.

We would do the sweat lodge in rounds which would extend 10 – 25 minutes in the lodge followed by time spent cooling off outside. It was blistering hot inside the lodge. Outside the temperature was 20 degrees above zero, a frosty night for Alabama. Inside the lodge, we passed around a talking stick. As it was passed around the circle, each person said a prayer, told a story, or shared some meaningful event in their life that happened recently. Sometimes someone might also share a vision they had experienced. That day, one person started by saying, "O sacred and mysterious one, we send up a voice. Come be with us, manifest yourself in our heart. Show us that we are all related."

I felt the tenderness of our Lord in my heart as we prayed. I felt connected with each person in that lodge, the connectedness of the Church, the connectedness of all humanity.

A Healing Vision

During the second round, almost from the moment I entered the lodge, a scene unfolded. I saw Christ standing beside a stream in the Smoky Mountains. Crystal clear water rolled over the stones, making a gurgling sound as it made its way downward. I saw Christ clothed and vested in deer skin; he had his hands opened and raised up in prayer and healing. From the openness between his arms *nowhetee,* the Cherokee word for healing or medicine, came from his open hands. As he did that, I felt a wind blow over me that I knew to be the wind of the Spirit.

I then saw the animals of the forest gather around this Christ who had his arms wide open in healing and blessing. The torn and hurt animals were made well and bounded off back into the woods. Then people surrounded him. I found myself standing next to him on the rock. I saw a deer wounded by an arrow, his pained face wrinkled in terror, who was having a difficult time breathing. I saw a three-year-old who had no one to love him and the look of dejection on his face. I saw some of my own pain, too. I saw myself as a young child when Daddy was in the midst of some of his delusions and threatened to kill me and slice me up with a knife. I remembered the terror of that and saw the stark fear on my young face in the vision.

Healing came from the arms of Christ lifted up in blessing, lifted up in healing. As the healing flowed, I saw the face of the rejected child soften and an ease come over that face. I felt in my heart that God was loving me and healing my past pain. I saw a widow who had just lost her husband standing there puzzled and dazed. Christ walked out to her and embraced her, saying, *Your husband may be gone for a while, but I can embrace you in his absence.*

I talked about my emerging vision with the people in the lodge. As I watched the vision, I saw the healing growing dim. Not so many were being healed now and I cried out, "O Great One, O Gentle One clothed in deer skin, why is the healing dimming?"

And the words came, *I do not choose to heal alone. I do not choose to work my medicine alone, but I call all of you to work with me. May your hands and feet connect with the world and with me so that you may be a conduit of the world's greatest medicine.*

Then I realized Christ wanted us to join him. So I lifted up my arms beside him and I told everyone in the lodge to lift up their hands. Christ said to us all in my vision, *For healing to flow, I need all of you to join with me, making a circle of hands entwined with hands. In the inner part of the circle, bless and pray for those who were wounded. Let the wounded stand in the center of your circle, those wounded in heart, wounded in body, wounded spiritually, wounded by not yet knowing my love.*

As I lifted up my arms and the others lifted up their arms,

I saw the healed deer scampering out into the woods. I saw children filled with pain and loneliness grow still and be peaceful. As the grace of healing which I received from Christ poured out from my heart, I could feel the pain of those in front of me. Healing was a connection that ran both ways.

As the healing diminished again, I heard Jesus say, *Let me bring to you some helpers in healing.* I saw those that loved me: my parents (even though we had hard times, they truly loved me); my grandparents; my Aunt Genella; and Margaret Cox, my teacher. All stood beside me. The strength that they had given me, the mystery they implanted within me, was part of how healing would come.

The Changing of Weapons

The healing diminished again. I heard Christ speaking again, *Now I will show you the hardest part of healing: the changing of weapons.*

The message puzzled me. "The changing of weapons"— what did this mean? Then in an instant I was standing there at the river and was yet in a totally different place in the way that such things can happen only in dreams and visions. The medicine that radiated from Christ carried me to a different place. I stood before a tree that reached high into the sky, towering so tall I could not see the top of it. I stood in awe of the tree and the image, and the symbol of the tree became clear to me. I thought of that great tree of peace that Bonaventure spoke of in his visionary meditation, "The Tree of Peace" (*Lignum Vitae*). His vast tree, he wrote, symbolized Christ, who came from the stump of Jesse. I thought of the Native symbol of the tree, the great tree of peace in the native prophet Deganawidah's vision. The tree that Christ brought me to symbolized both.

Under the branches, brilliantly shining, were what I can only call medicine stones, healing stone jewels that gave off a dazzling, healing light that radiated the healing of the eternal God. Christ said, *I will teach you the lesson of the changing of weapons.* He then reached, as it were, into the place between my heart and abdomen, that place where we feel our feelings, and drew out of me a weapon, a stone war club. Christ said, *Inside you hold many weapons. When you were a child, so much frightened you. The other face of fear is bitterness, the bitterness of weapons that would strike back, that would hurt others. Now reach in yourself and pull out the weapons.* I reached inside my heart and took out all sorts of knives and war clubs and arrows that came from me—the products of my hurt, the children of my fear, the weapons I used to strike back and hold off the fear. I drew them out of my vitals and placed them under the roots of the great tree that symbolized Jesus. There, they transformed into medicine stones that radiated great brilliance. I stood there for a season, removing the weapons from my soul and placing them in the roots of the tree of Jesse, the great tree of peace that alone can transfigure our anger and our fury.

Then in an instant I returned to the stone island in the middle of the river. This time I held a bright and shining medicine stone in the palm of each hand, and I could feel the warmth as my fingers gathered around the glowing stones. The glow of the stones flowed through my hand, through my limbs, through all of me as I stood on the rock with Christ.

This time the row of people in front of me had familiar faces. These were the people who, in my mind, had hurt me, the people toward whom I held both unfelt and felt anger. Among those who stood near were a teacher who had made fun of me, students who had laughed at me when I was growing up, and the people I would avoid if I saw them in a mall. All of them appeared before me now. My eyes wanted to turn away; I had held such weapons of harshness in me. I tried to let my heart reach out to them and let the healing rays flow from me. My limbs weakened and wavered as I looked at all the people of my pain. I could not look them in the eye. I saw not only the people who had hurt me but also the people I had hurt. I saw that I too had inflicted wounds. I could look at them and see and feel what my words and actions had done to them. Visible in their faces were the scars of my withdrawing myself from them and saying hard things to them. I could feel it all, and I collapsed inside.

I spoke out with the language of my heart, standing near Christ, who stood beside me: "I cannot do this by myself. I cannot go through this alone. I can do this only with your help."

Then I heard Christ say in the heart's wordless communion: *These are your greatest teachers, these people of your pain. These are your teachers in becoming a healer.* I stretched out my hands. I could look them in the face now and the healing again flowed not only to them but also to the whole multitude. My mind and my heart came back to the sweat lodge. I sat there on the ground, which was now moist with my sweat. Sweat poured down until my eyes burned with the salt. Tears streamed from my eyes. Stillness like eternity filled the lodge. I then told the others of my vision, which is really the vision of all of us. It is the vision that in some way every one of us has, if we will but stop a moment and see it.

I said to the group, "Let us now in silence all go to the root of the tree of life and begin changing our weapons into medicine stones, for we are all called to be healers, and this is the pathway of healers." After a long silence, we exited the lodge, letting the jolt of the freezing wind cool our heated, near-naked bodies. The wind quickly cooled us, and we gathered near the fire to warm from the cool. We then entered the lodge for another round. A few people prayed; some chanted. I sat in silence, and in the silence, without words, I heard Christ's message.

You cannot be healed without becoming a healer. Gather in all the love that you have known—the love of all those whose gaze became my gaze—all the touches, all the love that met you in creation. The ways of healing are the ways of touching and being touched; feeling the pain in some way as I feel it. I heal by inhabiting the deepest places of the deepest hurts. My healing is my calling, my calling to join in the healing of earth and sky.

Join me, all of you. Join me in the mending. I am the healer who loves and heals through many healers and the lover who loves through many who love. Change your weapons, the children of your pain, into medicine stones. Look in the eyes of the people of your pain. I am the one who ties together that which has been torn and mends that which has been ripped and wounded.

The world changed for a moment, caught up in an eternity of light. It sparkled, and I dwelled in the eternity of its sparkling. After this vision, each of us exited the lodge, returned to the old farmhouse, dressed, and began our journey home.

Chapter Nineteen

Dreams of the New Creation

In the past several years, I've had dreams of the new creation, of heaven, the time of all the consummation, the time all things will be brought together by God's love. Those dreams are beyond words, but what I most felt in them was a sense of love. They did not involve going into a place or time that was foreign, but one that was deeply familiar where everything was imbued with the presence of God. There was a meeting, a reunion, with that which had been lost, a feeling of old friends and family. There was also a sense that unspeakable horrors like the holocaust were cast aside and instead the harmony of God prevailed. It was the world we know now, but looked at through God's eternal perspective.

In those visions and dreams, I saw hands holding hands and dancing, smiles, laughter, happiness, and all God had created. What was lost was restored. What was forgotten was remembered. God was not so much an object to be seen but the very ground of our existence. As I try very feebly to write the information of this dream, I feel a message forming within me. I will try to put it into words that can be understood. This is inadequate, I know. As St. Paul wrote, "It is though we see through a glass darkly." Yet, we see. We still see. (1 Cor 13:12)

The New Jerusalem, Heaven, is Rushing Toward You

The voice says, *My children, I told you I would have a place, a mansion, prepared for you when I called you to my bosom. It is not strange, wild, unlike earth, but rather earth and life living as God would have them; as I would have them.*

My children, glory is coming. The new creation, the new Jerusalem, heaven is rushing toward you. Glory is not so much streets paved with gold or houses roofed with diamonds. Instead, it is like those moments in your life when you struggled in a relationship until a time came when you both forgave the other and you both felt God at the same time. It is like when you turned from destructive patterns and asked God's assistance to help you with behavior you could no longer handle yourself, perhaps a struggle with alcohol, drugs, or other addictions. In those moments of desperation, God entered into your hurt and you felt heaven.

Heaven is a place where your disabilities no longer weigh you down, where sin no longer weighs you down, for your sins are profoundly forgiven by the great coach of heaven, Jesus. It is in the great and profound moments of everyday existence that you taste the everlasting. It is the healing of this earth, this world, and of glory shining upon the ordinary so that it glows with a divine presence.

I Can Infuse You with Wonder

I stand ready to take your hand, to infuse you with a wonder, a joy that makes earthly things and earthly memories pure and touched by the amazement of eternity. It is in the stuff of daily life transfixed and transformed that heaven will come to be. I can eternally redeem that which was lost and put together what was missing. Glory, heaven, the new creation is like seeing again through the eyes of the toddler when everything is utterly fascinating, utterly fresh, and capable of communicating the presence of the light that transforms the ordinary into the holy.

My children, see with new eyes. See the depth and the freshness of each smile you see, of each smell you smell, of each taste you taste. Taste the inherent glory that is in those things for I have given you eyes that can see wonder. I have given you eyes that can turn the world into one great astonishment.

Have you ever driven in the midst of very high mountains with the mist all around them and heard the scene before you, as it were, express mystery and eternity, aching with the beauty that words cannot express? Heaven is life turned into that beauty, real human life as real and earthly as an unconsecrated host and wine which are consecrated by glory and become the wondrous drink and meal of the Resurrection. Abandon yourself to me and I will give you a taste of glory.

Your Lives are like a Tapestry

In many ways the new creation, heaven, glory is like a beautiful tapestry. If you look on the back side of a tapestry, all you see are different colored dangling strings in no particular order. That's how your lives are. They are tied and knotted up. They are somewhat incoherent at times. The pattern is not readily available. But if you reverse it and look at the front, you see the beautiful picture depicted by the tapestry. Right now you see the struggles and the disconnectedness. You see the loose strings. But, in eternity, the tapestry will be turned over and you will see the front and see how it looks from my eyes and see the beautifully woven tapestry forever dwelling in the timelessness of my eternity.

Endnotes

[1] George W. Cornell, "Spiritual Experiences Defy Scientific Beliefs," *Daily News Los Angeles*, Saturday, 10 January 1987, Valley section, p. 18.

[2] "St. Thomas Aquinas," *Internet Encyclopedia of Philosophy*, http://www.iep.utm.edu/aquinas/

[3] St. Augustine, *City of God*, Book Twenty-Two, Chapter Eight, http://www.newadvent.org/fathers/120122.htm

[4] Dr. Dean Hamer, *The God Gene: How Faith is Hardwired into Our Genes* (New York: Anchor, 2005).

[5] See Eddie Ensley, *Visions: The Soul's Path to the Holy* (Chicago: Loyola Press, 2000) 52-66, 91-92.

[6] William Mcintosh, "A Theater That Transforms Us," *Parabola*, winter 1997, electronic edition, Northern Light Database.

[7] The following is an excerpt from Paragraph 14 of *Verbum Domini*. The full document can be found at http://w2.vatican.va/content/benedict-xvi/en/apost_exhortations/documents/hf_ben-xvi_exh_20100930_verbum-domini.html

Consequently the Synod pointed to the need to "help the faithful to distinguish the word of God from private revelations"[44] whose role "is not to 'complete' Christ's definitive revelation, but to help live more fully by it in a certain period of history".[45] The value of private revelations is essentially different from that of the one public revelation: the latter demands faith; in it God himself speaks to us through human words and the mediation of the living community of the Church. The criterion for judging the truth of a private revelation is its orientation to Christ himself. If it leads us away from him, then it certainly does not come from the Holy Spirit, who guides us more deeply into the Gospel, and not away from it. Private revelation is an aid to this faith, and it demonstrates its credibility precisely because it refers back to the one public revelation. Ecclesiastical approval of a private revelation essentially means that its message contains nothing contrary to faith and morals; it is licit to make it public and the faithful are authorized to give to it their prudent adhesion. A private revelation can introduce new emphases, give rise to new forms of piety, or deepen older ones. It can have a certain prophetic character (cf. *1 Th* 5:19-21) and can be a valuable aid for better understanding and living the Gospel at a certain time; consequently it should not be treated lightly. It is a help which is proffered, but its use is not obligatory. In any event, it must be a matter of nourishing faith, hope and love, which are for everyone the permanent path of salvation.[46]

[8] Sylvia Carey, *Jolted Sober* (Los Angeles: Lowell House, 1989).

[9] Thomas á Kempis, *The Imitation of Christ*, trans. Joseph E. Tylenda (New York: Vintage Books, 1998) 83.

[10] Ibid, 75.

[11] Bernard Gui, *The Life of St. Thomas Aquinas*, ed. and trans, Kenelm Foster, O.P., contained in *The Life of St. Thomas: Biographical Documents* (Baltimore: Helicon Press, 1959) 37.

[12] Simon Tugwell, ed., *Albert and Thomas: Selected Writings* (Classics of Western Spirituality) (New York: Paulist Press, 1988) 380.

[13] Bernard Gui, *The Life of St. Thomas Aquinas*, ed. and trans, Kenelm Foster, O.P., contained in *The Life of St. Thomas: Biographical Documents* (Baltimore: Helicon Press, 1959) 37.

[14] St. Augustine, *Ennarationes in Psalmos 97,* translation Abbott David Geraets O.S.B, 4—PL 37, 1254-1255.

[15] https://w2.vatican.va/content/john-paul-ii/en/speeches/1987/september/ documents/hf_jp-ii_spe_19870914_amerindi-phoenix.html

About the Author

Eddie Ensley is a Catholic permanent deacon (clergyman) from the diocese of Savannah, Georgia. He is part of the clergy staff at St. Anne Church in Columbus, Georgia. He teaches graduate school at Josephinum Diaconate Institute, Pontifical College Josephinum and is also a course developer for that Institute. He is also part of Deacons in Ministry, an official Catholic organization approved by his diocese and the United States Conference of Catholic Bishops. In addition, he is a mission member of the Alleluia Community, also in Georgia.

Deacon Ensley is a NCCA licensed clinical pastoral counselor with a master's degree in pastoral studies (Loyola University) and a doctorate in clinical pastoral counseling (Cornerstone University). He reaches around 27 thousand people a year through leading retreats, parish missions, and clergy (deacon) retreats throughout North America. He is of Native American descent on both sides of his family and an enrolled Echota Cherokee.

Parish Missions, Retreats, and Conferences

The author of this book, Deacon Eddie Ensley, along with Deacon Robert Herrmann, offers parish missions, retreats, and conferences throughout the country. A parish mission by the two deacons draws the whole parish together. It recharges the congregation. Everyone takes time for the truly important things like wonder, mystery, healing, and prayer. People are reconciled. Faith is awakened. Vocations are discovered.

The deacons can also lead clergy retreats and conferences as well as religious education conferences. To bring them to your parish or your event or to ask for an information packet about what their retreats and conferences can offer your area, you can visit their website www.parishmission.net, or email Deacon Ensley at pmissions@charter.net.

"The Mission proved to be a tremendous help for our families… Our attendance was better than ever. The guided meditations throughout were vivid and uplifting. The parish mission was filled with solid content. The greatest compliment has been in the attendance."

— Father John T. Euker, St. John the Baptist,
Perryopolis, Pennsylvania

Additional Books by Deacon Eddie Ensley, Ph.D.

Finding Inner Peace (23rd Publications, 2017)
Love Your Neighbor (Franciscan Media, 2015)
Step-by-Step Spirituality for Deacons
(Abbey Press, 2014)
Glimpsing the Glory (23rd Publications, 2012)
Everyday Mysticism (23rd Publications, 2012)
*Healing the Soul – Finding Peace and Consolation
When Life Hurts* (23rd Publications, 2013)
Prayer that Relieves Stress and Worry
(Contemplative Books, 2007)
Letters From Jesus – Experiencing the Depth of His Love
(23rd Publications, 2011)
Writing to be Whole - A Healing Journal
(Loyola Press, 2001)
Visions – The Soul's Path to the Sacred
(Loyola Press, 2000)
Prayer that Heals Our Emotions (Harper/Collins, 1988)
Sounds of Wonder (Paulist Press, 1977, reprinted 2013)

79131019R00066

Made in the USA
Middletown, DE
07 July 2018